GREAT CRIME BUSTERS

True Stories of Crime Detection

A skillful crime reporter tells about ten crimes that were prevented or solved, including the plot to murder Abraham Lincoln before he took office. Half the crimes solved in these tales were broken by the work of amateur sleuths, usually young men. The other half were solved through the methods that account for 99 percent of all solved crimes — painstaking footwork by tireless policemen. All except two were published in *Boys' Life* magazine and were chosen for this book by the editors of *Boys' Life*.

Swallow and King

GREAT CRIME BUSTERS

by Alan Hynd

Illustrated by Albert Orbaan

G. P. Putnam's Sons **New York**

© 1967 by Boy Scouts of America
By permission of *Boys' Life* Magazine, owned
and published by Boy Scouts of America
All rights reserved
Published simultaneously in the Dominion of Can-
ada by Longmans Canada Limited, Toronto
Library of Congress Catalog Card Number: 67–24143
PRINTED IN THE UNITED STATES OF
AMERICA

The Other Plot to Kill Lincoln, copyright 1966 by
author, published in *Reader's Digest,* February, 1966.

Voices from the Grave, copyright by author, originally published as The Case of the Voices from the Grave
in *True,* The Man's Magazine, August, 1955.

All other stories in this book were originally published
in *Boys' Life* magazine.

Contents

GREAT CRIME BUSTERS

The Man with the Camera Eyes

Not long ago, the New York Police Department boasted one of the most unique detectives in the whole history of law-enforcement—a man known to the police and the underworld of two continents as Camera Eyes. His real name was Henry Oswald; he was a big athletic man with a pleasant, though knowing, face and mild blue eyes behind gold-rimmed glasses. His eyes were literally cameras; Detective Oswald never forgot a face. Sometimes, walking along a crowded street or sitting in the grandstand at Yankee Stadium, he would spot fugitives from justice whom he hadn't seen in years. The sleuth was never able to explain, even to himself, his phenomenal memory for faces.

9

Some time back, Detective Oswald was down in Montevideo, Uruguay, on an extradition matter when, taking a walk late one night before retiring, he was accosted by a sailor who asked him for a light for his cigarette. As Detective Oswald obliged, striking a match and holding it up to the sailor's cigarette, he studied the fellow's face from force of habit. The sailor was light-complexioned, blue-eyed, round of face, and altogether quite pleasant looking. He thanked the detective and went on his way. Both, naturally, thought no more of the incident.

Two years later, far from Montevideo—in Brooklyn, home of the Dodgers—there was an armed holdup. A light-complexioned, good-looking man of about twenty-five, sharply dressed in a tight-fitting black overcoat with a velvet collar and wearing a derby at a jaunty angle, walked into a little stationery store on Bleecker Street with a revolver in his right hand. He held up the proprietor, an aged man named Samuel Walters; during the crime, Mr. Walters' wife, drawn to the store from living quarters in the rear, got a good look at the fellow. So did several residents of the neighborhood, as the criminal, still waving his gun, darted along Bleecker Street, ducked into an alley, and disappeared from view.

Next day, acting on a description of the criminal furnished by the victim, his wife and several others who had seen the fellow, Brooklyn detectives went to the home of a youth of twenty-five by the name of Jimmy

Campbell, and arrested him. Campbell was taken to the precinct station and placed in a lineup with a group of assorted felons. Then the holdup witnesses were brought in to see if they could pick out the culprit. The victim and his wife and five residents of the neighborhood unhesitatingly picked Campbell.

Campbell, a mild-mannered chap who was something of a neighborhood celebrity as a sandlot baseball player, had an alibi. At the hour of the crime he claimed to have been across the East River in Manhattan, standing in a line in front of an employment agency. Campbell had not obtained work, however, nor had he known anybody in the employment line; thus he couldn't prove his alibi.

Camera Eyes Oswald was assigned to talk to Jimmy Campbell and to try to get a confession from him. Oswald was startled when he walked into the prisoner's cell. "We've met before," were his opening words to Campbell. "Where?" asked Campbell.

"Down in Montevideo," said Camera Eyes. "You stopped me on the street there two years ago and asked me for a match. You were in the Navy."

"I was in the Navy, all right, but I was never in Montevideo."

"Come now," said Oswald, "we're not going to get anywhere if you're going to lie. Why don't you admit what you've done?"

"But I tell you I didn't commit that crime. I was trying to find a job that afternoon."

Detective Oswald was walking to his car parked outside the jail when a young fellow of about sixteen stopped him and asked, "You're the detective who's going to send Jimmy Campbell to prison, aren't you?"

Oswald, curious, stopped. "Are you a friend of Jimmy?" he asked.

"Yes, sir. Jimmy didn't hold up that man."

"How do you know, young fellow?"

"He just couldn't have done it, sir. That's all I know; he just couldn't have done it."

"You'd have to have more proof than just a belief in Jimmy Campbell's innocence, you know."

Oswald got into his car. Before he put the car into motion, he glanced at the chap, standing on the sidewalk looking in his direction. His camera eyes took a photograph of Jimmy Campbell's young friend. That night, Camera Eyes saw the photograph of the trusting boy who, for some reason or other, had supreme faith in the fellow charged with such a serious crime. What, wondered Detective Oswald, had inspired such faith? Obviously, Campbell was guilty; the victim himself and six other reputable citizens had positively identified him. And Campbell was lying in his teeth when he said that he had never been in Montevideo. Or was he?

The Navy records, usually complete and very detailed, were incomplete and not at all detailed concerning Jimmy Campbell's exact whereabouts on the date when Detective Oswald had lit the cigarette for the sailor in Montevideo. Campbell had been on a ship in South American waters at the time in question, but exactly what ship wasn't clear. He had been transferred from one ship to another during the period in question, and his record had been misfiled. All the indications were, however, that he could very well have been on shore leave in Montevideo the night Camera Eyes had studied the sailor's face while lighting his cigarette.

Detective Oswald spent a little time with Jimmy Campbell in the Brooklyn jail each day. A grand jury had indicted Campbell for the holdup of Samuel Walters; if ever a man was headed straight for prison, Campbell was. He continued to protest his innocence, however; continued to insist not only that he had not been in Brooklyn when the the crime was committed, but that he had never set foot in the city of Montevideo.

One day, when Detective Oswald called to conduct another questioning session, he learned that Campbell had just been taken to a hospital. He had slashed his wrists in his cell in an attempt at suicide—a classic indication, under the circumstances, of guilt.

When Camera Eyes walked out of the jail that day, the young man who had previously exhibited such faith in Campbell was waiting for him. "I know what you're thinking, sir," he said. "You're thinking Jimmy Campbell tried to commit suicide because he was guilty."

"What else can I think, young fellow?" asked Oswald. The detective grew suddenly thoughtful. "Say," he suggested, "what do you say you and I go around the corner and have a banana split?" That was fine with the boy, who identified himself as Bill Hoffman.

"How long," asked Detective Oswald of Bill Hoffman, as the two tackled their banana splits, "have you known Jimmy Campbell?"

"For about three years, sir."

"And just why do you think he's such a wonderful fellow?"

"Well, sir, I broke a window last year by hitting a home run through it. I didn't have the money to pay for the window, and the man who owned the house was goin' to come around and tell my father when Jimmy Campbell heard about it. He gave me the money to pay the man so my father wouldn't know about it."

As Bill Hoffman ate his banana split, he detailed other acts of kindness of the fellow ticketed for prison—how he had bought baseball bats and other equipment for the guys in the neighborhood when it was fairly obvious he didn't have much money to spare; how, very late one night, he had heard that a mother of one of the young players needed some rare medicine, obtainable at that hour only across the river in Manhattan, and had gone to get it himself. Things like that.

"Well," said Oswald when the splits were finished and he got into his car for the drive to his squad headquarters, "we'll see what turns up."

In his time, Camera Eyes had known many people who had vested blind faith in criminals. Somehow,

15

though, the faith of Bill Hoffman in Jimmy Campbell was different. Here was a fellow who, despite his comparative youth, struck the detective as an instinctive judge of character. He would be unlikely to be fooled by the surface behavior of a man who was evil at heart. Then, too, the acts of kindness on the part of Jimmy Campbell that Bill Hoffman had related hardly seemed compatible with the makeup of a man who would be capable of premeditated crime.

Weeks passed. Jimmy Campbell recovered from his attempt at suicide and was returned to jail. His trial was to come up in about a month. Then there came some routine intelligence from the Chicago police to the New York police. A man of twenty-five, named Jesse Reklaw, had been picked up in Chicago while trying to pawn some valuable jewelry stolen during a robbery in the town of Mattoon, Illinois—some two hundred miles from the Windy City. When arrested, Reklaw had been found to possess a diary—a diary in which he had recorded, just for his own information, a long record of robberies in several cities, including New York. Chicago thought New York might like to take a look at the diary. The Reklaw record was not divided up into days, but into weeks. During one week, a couple of months previously, Reklaw had made the laconic notation:

> Well, I guess I got
> away with that job in
> Brooklyn.

16

THE MAN WITH THE CAMERA EYES

The diary was turned over to Camera Eyes for examination. What job did the entry in the diary refer to?

Detective Oswald closed the diary. Then the picture of the trusting, earnest face of Bill Hoffman flashed into his mind's-eye. So far as Bill Hoffman was concerned, somebody had gotten away with a job in Brooklyn—the crime for which his friend Jimmy Campbell was charged. Oswald opened the diary again. He noticed that the got-away-with-it Brooklyn entry had been made during the week of the holdup of Samuel Walters.

Detective Oswald found himself racked by conflict. Here he had a case in Brooklyn all wrapped up, until this young man named Bill Hoffman had come along to put doubt in his mind. Should he go out to Illinois to question this fellow Jesse Reklaw—go on what could very well be a wild goose chase—just because Bill Hoffman, in spite of the evidence given by the victim and six other reputable witnesses against Jimmy Campbell, said Campbell couldn't possibly be guilty? Camera Eyes looked again and again in his mind's eye at that trusting, intelligent face of Bill Hoffman and pondered anew the good deeds ascribed to Jimmy Campbell by young Hoffman. Within an hour, he was on a plane for Illinois.

If Oswald had been startled on walking into the Brooklyn jail and seeing Jimmy Campbell for the first time, he was doubly startled when he walked into the jail in the town of Mattoon, looked through the bars of a cell and laid eyes on Jess Reklaw for the first time.

Detective Oswald might as well have been looking at Jimmy Campbell's twin. The prisoner in Brooklyn and the prisoner in Mattoon were the same age, the same height, the same approximate weight, and had the same blond complexions, blue eyes and round, pleasant countenances. Reklaw even had a chesterfield coat, as Campbell had, and a derby. Oswald saw at once that because of the almost unbelievable similarity in appearance between the two men, plus the strange coincidence that they had dressed alike, the victim and the other witnesses could easily have mistaken Jimmy Campbell for Jesse Reklaw.

Camera Eyes did not speak to Reklaw for a little while. He just stood outside the bars looking at him. Now, for the first time, he realized a basic difference between Campbell and Reklaw, despite their many similarities. Reklaw had mean eyes; Campbell didn't. Campbell could look a man straight in the face; Reklaw could not.

Oswald asked to be let into the cell. He thought of Bill Hoffman, the trusting young man who had hit a home run through a window, and told himself if it had not been for that, and other incidents seemingly unrelated to crime, a hideous miscarriage of justice might have taken place in Brooklyn. For Camera Eyes Oswald was certain, as certain as he had ever been of anything that he was entering the cell of the fellow who had stuck up Samuel Walters.

"Well, Walker," Oswald began to the prisoner, "you're sure in a fine jam."

"What do you mean calling me Walker? That's not my name."

"Reklaw is Walker spelled backward. That's old stuff, Walker, trying to hide your real identity by changing your name. But that's beside the point; tell me, when did you get out of the Navy?"

Jess Walker stiffened.

"The Navy? How did you know I was in the Navy?"

The detective ignored the question. He was measuring the prisoner. Oswald's two statements out of the blue—the prisoner's real name and the fact that he had been in the Navy—had knocked Walker off balance. A good detective senses the propitious moment to rush in for a quick knockout.

"Two years ago," Camera Eyes continued, "when you were in the Navy, you were on shore leave in Montevideo one night and you stopped a man on the street and asked him for a match. Think hard, Walker, and you'll remember that. It wasn't so long ago—only two years."

Jesse Walker's eyes widened as he stared at Oswald. "How do you know all this stuff about me? What are you, a magician?"

The detective was calm in contrast to Walker's rising turmoil. "It's my business to know everything about you, Walker," he went on.

"I know, for instance, that you stuck up an old man named Samuel Walters on Bleecker Street in Brooklyn nine weeks and three days ago."

"You what!"

"You're not very smart, Walker, you've just been lucky up to now. Another fellow who looks like you might have gone to prison for your crime, but he won't now—thanks to a young man who had faith in him."

"What do you mean by that?"

"It's something you wouldn't understand, Walker. But as I was saying, you're not very smart. You *had* to write everything down in a diary!"

Jesse Walker confessed to the Brooklyn crime. He went to prison for it. Jimmy Campbell was, of course, released—the victim of a stranger-than-fiction set of coincidences, yet the recipient of a priceless faith on the part of a young friend. Detective Oswald got Jimmy Campbell a good job. One of the first things Campbell did was to seek out Bill Hoffman. "Listen, Bill," he said with a grin, "if you ever hit any more home runs through windows, let me know. I'll be glad to pay for them."

Menace in the Mail

Half a dozen grave-visaged men sat around an oval conference table in a room in the main Philadelphia post office late on the morning of Good Friday, April 10, 1936. Their eyes were focused on a quietly-dressed man of middle age at the head of the table—J. W. Johnston, Chief of the Philadelphia Division of the United States Postal Inspection Service.

"Gentlemen," said Chief Johnston to six of the most seasoned Postal Inspectors in the Division, "we have a murderer on our hands. He has killed three people out in Wilkes-Barre within the past hour, by infernal machines sent through the mails. You are to leave for Wilkes-Barre at once and find him."

21

Chief Johnston glanced at some notes he had jotted down while the postmaster of Wilkes-Barre, a city west of Philadelphia in the heart of the great Pennsylvania anthracite coal region, had long-distanced him to report the known facts. "A miner named Thomas Maloney," Chief Johnston said, "received a cigar box through the mails. It exploded when he opened it, and killed him and his seven-year-old son. Another man—a cemetery caretaker by the name of Michael Gallagher—met death the same way."

A third cigar box had been received by one Luther Kniffen, an undertaker. The mortician had pried it open from the rear, rather than from the front. For that reason, an infernal device within had failed to explode.

"The Wilkes-Barre police have the unexploded device," said Chief Johnston. "Run down every clue it offers, if it takes five years."

The Postal Inspectors arrived in Wilkes-Barre early in the afternoon. They saw at a glance that the component parts of the unexploded infernal device, the box in which it had been sent, and the paper in which the box had been wrapped, were so common as to be discouragingly untraceable. String or twine, usually utilized to wrap packages, and which is often so distinctive that it can be run down to its source, had been carefully avoided by the murderer. The outer wrapping of the package had been secured by glue. The address was in pencil, and fashioned of block letters obviously contrived to deceive.

The absence of clues was in itself a clue. Here was a killer possessed of intelligence. Here was a man cold and deliberate, who figured out everything carefully in advance.

The infernal device consisted of two ordinary dry-cell batteries, sold everywhere, and a piece of dynamite common in the coal country. The batteries had been fastened to the dynamite by ordinary copper wire in such a way that when the cigar box was opened from the front, the wire would be pulled taut, producing sparks from the batteries to explode the dynamite. The dynamite and the batteries were neatly held in place by several small pieces of pine slat that looked as if they had come from a vegetable crate and which had been sawed to measure.

Postal Inspectors are authorities on infernal devices. The average non-expert on explosives, they knew from experience, was profligate in the use of dynamite when constructing a lethal contraption.

This killer had been far from profligate; he had, in fact, been niggardly. He had put just enough of the explosive in the cigar box to kill a person in close proximity to it.

Thus there emerged more information about the murderer. He was an expert with dynamite. He was a penny pincher. It wasn't that those two qualities in a man would make him stand out in this instance. Dynamite experts in the anthracite fields, where a knowledge of the explosive is almost a prerequisite to earning a livelihood, lived virtually on every street. So did people who had to watch their pennies. Little had been revealed thus far.

Uncle Sam's detectives now concentrated on the rooms in which Maloney, the miner, and Gallagher, the cemetery caretaker, had opened the boxes and met their deaths. By the tedious process of sorting the debris, the investigators gathered up parts of the wrapping paper that had covered the packages, pieces of the cigar boxes, and some of the small pieces of pine slats used to hold the parts of the infernal devices in place. There was glue on the retrieved wrapping paper. Pieces of cigar-box wood from the Maloney home, when matched up jigsaw fashion, disclosed a trademark that was the same as that on the box received by the undertaker. It was therefore assumed that the box that had been sent to Gallagher had borne the same trademark.

The brand of cigar in question was an expensive one. There was little call for it in the coal regions. The investigators regarded this as a hopeful clue. If they found a man who smoked this particular cigar, they just might have their murderer.

Kniffen, the undertaker, couldn't account for the fact

that he had been marked for death. He couldn't explain, either, just why it was that he had pried the cigar box open from the back rather than from the front. Finally, he laid his act to absent-mindedness.

The investigators began to wonder if there was any significance in the fact that two of the three men marked for death were associated with cemeteries—one as a caretaker and another as an undertaker. It did seem strange, that of all the people in a city of almost 90,000, two of the three people included in a death plot had something to do with cemeteries.

Gallagher, the caretaker, had been a man in his late sixties—kindly, generous and devout. Maloney, the murdered miner, was the type of man the newspapers refer to as having no known enemies. But Gallagher and Maloney, and Kniffen, had had at least one enemy, and a mortal one at that. The problem was to find one man who had, either for the same or for varied reasons, borne a burning hatred toward all three.

Good Friday is a religious holiday that means a great deal to Catholics and Protestants alike. It means more to a Catholic, however, than it means to a non-Catholic. Good Friday is one of the holiest of all days to one of the Catholic faith. While murderers are of all faiths, it seemed inconceivable to the investigators that this killer had been a Catholic. The religious training of a Catholic, regardless of the fact that he may have strayed from the fold, would in all probability have stayed his hand at such a crime as murder during the Holy Season.

Thus the sleuths were in possession of still another piece of information about the killer. He was probably a non-Catholic.

The three cigar boxes had been deposited in a United States mailbox near the center of the city the previous night between seven thirty and eleven o'clock. This was established through the mail carrier who made collections from the box at the hours in question. He clearly recalled having collected three heavy packages, the size of cigar boxes, on the eleven o'clock pickup. This meant that they had been dropped sometime after the seven-thirty pickup. Time was narrowing down.

The box in which the infernal devices had been posted was near a Lutheran church. There had been Holy Week services in the church the night before—between the hours of the pickups and the hours of the services. Capable detectives make a note of everything, however.

It developed that Luther Kniffen, the lucky one of the trio marked for death, had formerly been the Sheriff of Luzerne County, in which Wilkes-Barre is located. This forthwith opened a new avenue of investigation. A sheriff in the pursuit of his official duties would more than likely have incurred the enmity of many men. The key to the riddle lay in locating a man who mortally

hated the former sheriff, and who felt the same way toward Maloney, the miner, and Gallagher, the cemetery watchman.

Sheriff's records disclosed that a miner named Michael Fugman had, a few years previously, been arrested for disorderly conduct and that Michael Gallagher, the cemetery watchman, had been a witness against him. Where Tom Maloney, the dead miner, had fitted into the picture, if indeed there had been a picture that had any bearing on the murders, wasn't apparent.

Michael Fugman, a native of Germany, was a man of fifty who had both staunch friends and bitter enemies. He was a stocky, taciturn individual, quick with his fists in arguments with fellow miners. He was just as quick to go to a man who was in trouble and say, "You better let me lend you a hundred; pay me back when you can."

Michael Fugman was, at the moment, in a hospital. He had been seriously injured in a mine cave-in, since the investigation into the murders began. Investigators were told that the patient was too ill to be questioned.

Certain facts tended to place Fugman in the murder picture. He was a non-Catholic. He was highly intelligent. He was a member of the Lutheran Church which was situated near the mailbox where the death packages had been mailed. He had attended services with relatives in the church the night the packages were mailed.

There were weightier facts on the other side of the investigative ledger. While the killer had been an expert with dynamite, Fugman, unlike most miners, was mortally afraid to use explosive. Fellow workers had long known of his fear.

Fugman did not seem to be a man to hold a grudge. The investigators learned that he had gone to the home of Mike Gallagher, the man who had testified against him, only a few months previously, and offered the hand of friendship.

Most certainly Fugman was an unlikely suspect so far as the murder of Tom Maloney went. Maloney had been in financial trouble a year before. Fugman had gone to him and offered him the loan of several hundred dollars. Maloney had refused. Fugman had forced the money on him.

Fugman's reputation for generosity didn't square with the deduction that the murderer, niggardly with his dynamite, had been a penny pincher. So far as normal possession of cigar boxes went, Fugman didn't smoke cigars. Smokers of the expensive brand of cigars, trademarked on the murder debris, were being gradually eliminated one by one.

Chief Johnston, in Philadelphia, pondered the reports on Michael Fugman being sent in by the Inspectors in the murder locale. Chief Johnston was a man who took nothing for granted. He dispatched an agent to Germany to peer into Fugman's background.

The intelligence from abroad was electrifying. Fugman had been seriously injured in Germany not long before departing for the United States. He had been injured in a dynamite blast. He had been an expert with dynamite. The fact that he had been injured by dynamite had caused him to shy away from the explosive after he had gone to the Pennsylvania anthracite fields. Thus, he had been regarded as a person who knew nothing about dynamite when, in fact, he was an authority on the subject.

Chief Johnston ordered his men to canvass every cigar store in Wilkes-Barre. The agents thus came into possession of the information that not long before the infernal devices had been sent through the mails, a man had gone into a chain cigar store and asked the clerk if he had any dummies, a dummy being an empty cigar box for display purposes. The clerk had given the man several dummies. The dummies had borne the same trademark as the cigar-box debris retrieved from the Maloney home. The man to whom the clerk had given the dummies answered the general description of Michael Fugman. A photograph of Fugman was obtained from a Wilkes-Barre photographer who had made a portrait of the miner a year previously. The cigar-store clerk was unable to make a positive identification.

Fugman's home was secretly searched. In the cellar the Postal men found some pine slats from a vegetable crate, similar to those used to hold the component parts of the infernal devices in place. The cellar also yielded a quantity of brown paper similar to that used to wrap the death packages, and a pot of glue.

The glue and the paper were subjected to chemical analysis. Each was found to have precisely the same composition as the opposite numbers in the debris from the death blasts.

Now the Government sleuths questioned the relatives with whom Fugman had gone to the Lutheran church near the mail box where the packages were dropped the night before the murders. The relatives disclosed that Fugman had absented himself from the church during the services, saying he had a headache and wanted fresh air. He had been gone long enough to have driven to his home, less than a mile away, gotten the packages, mailed them and returned to the church.

People to whom Fugman had lent money were questioned. There now emerged an entirely different picture from that of a man who helped his fellow men when they were in financial distress. Fugman charged exorbitant rates of interest on money he pressed on people. It developed that Tom Maloney, the murdered miner, had fallen behind in his loan repayments to Fugman, and that Fugman had been unsuccessfully pressing him to pay up.

Fugman's show of friendship to Gallagher, the man who had testified against him on the occasion of his arrest, was now marked down as a cunningly contrived

31

empty gesture, by a killer bent on diverting suspicion from himself in advance.

Chief Johnston summoned his Inspectors to Philadelphia for an all-night conference. Michael Fugman was the killer, all right. Revenge had motivated him in mailing death packages to Kniffen, who had, while sheriff, arrested him, and Gallagher, who had testified against him. He had murdered Tom Maloney because of a bad debt.

There was considerable evidence—much of it spread out on the conference table—linking Michael Fugman to the terrible deeds. He was the type of man who could have conceived and executed such a crime. On the night before the murders, Fugman had been in the vicinity of the mail box where the death packages were dropped, during the hours when they had been dropped, and he had created for himself the opportunity to mail them unobserved. The physical evidence—the wrapping paper, the glue and the pieces of slat from a vegetable crate—pointed an incriminating finger at Fugman.

"Yet there is," Chief Johnston was saying to his men, "one thing we still lack—a piece of evidence that could have originated with Fugman, and Fugman alone. All the evidence we have, as incriminating as it is, could be successfully attacked by a clever lawyer. A lawyer could say—and we'd have a hard job disproving him—that all of our evidence, while it fits Fugman, could also fit somebody else we have not uncovered. No, gentlemen, we must lay hands on a piece of evidence that is not open to the slightest doubt—something as incontrovertible as a fingerprint."

The gaze of one of the Inspectors came to rest on the pine slats from the infernal devices and from Fugman's cellar. "Why not send those pieces," suggested the Inspector, "to the United States Forest Products Laboratory out in Madison, Wisconsin? I've heard that they perform miracles with wood there."

"An excellent idea," said Chief Johnston. "Perhaps the Forest Products Laboratory can supply us with the very evidence we lack."

Microscopic markings on the slats from the infernal devices and the slats from Fugman's cellar were compared in the Government laboratory in Wisconsin. The first conclusion arrived at was that all the slats had come from the same log. The grains matched precisely.

The second piece of incontrovertible evidence to develop under the microscope was that all the slats had been cut by the same saw in the sawmill. Saw scratches on the sides of the slats found in Fugman's cellar matched saw marks on the slats in the infernal devices.

A third piece of evidence—the clincher—revolved around marks made by a handsaw. Handsaw marks on the ends of the slats from the murder boxes matched perfectly with handsaw marks on the ends of sawed slats in the murderer's home. A saw taken from

Fugman's cellar made similar marks on pine slats from various sources, selected at random.

One day, months after the murders, with Fugman safely in jail, Chief Johnston once more sat at the conference table with the Inspectors who had solved the Wilkes-Barre horror. "I've written a letter of appreciation to the United States Forest Products Laboratory," he was telling his men. "Without the evidence that was developed for us out there, I doubt that Michael Fugman would ever have been convicted of his ruthless crimes."

Master Counterfeiters

The Chief of the United States Secret Service glanced up from his desk in the Treasury Building in Washington at the small sandy-haired young man who had just entered—Billy Burns, ace sleuth of the organization. He handed Burns a one-hundred-dollar bill, bearing a likeness of President Monroe. "Burns," said the Chief, "I want you to tell me if that is a genuine bill or a counterfeit."

Burns, an authority on spurious currency, pronounced the bill genuine.

"That shows you what a tough job you're in for," said the Chief. "That bill is a counterfeit. You are to find out who made it."

Several of the century notes had shown up in Philadelphia. The paper on which they were printed was an alarming reproduction of Uncle Sam's secret-formula stock, even to the red and blue silk threads distributed through it. The engraving was masterly. A money counter in a Quaker City bank had discovered the first of the bills when the red ink on the seal had smudged his dampened thumb. The lack of fastness of the red ink was the sole imperfection in what, up to then, was the most dangerous example of the so-called art of the counterfeiter ever encountered by the guardians of the Government's monetary medium.

Arriving in Philadelphia, Burns saw to it that the case received plenty of newspaper publicity, even to the detail of the non-fast red ink. The psychology here was to throw fear into the counterfeiters, thus causing them to cease shoving the queer, as the operation of passing bogus money is termed. Additionally, Burns calculated that the criminals would abandon the Monroe-head bill altogether and start work on a different issue. That would take time, and the Secret Service ace hoped to track down his quarry before a second threat could be launched on the country's monetary system.

There were many printing and engraving plants in the nation's third largest city where the bills could have been turned out. Burns had a hunch that the counterfeiters had originated in one of them. He assigned twenty agents to screen employees of the establishments in the hope of turning up somebody who might fit into the crime picture.

Burns himself went to New York, ninety miles distant. There he began the rounds of firms that supplied most of the Philadelphia printing and engraving houses with such basic needs as copper, etching acids, paper and ink. He wanted to know just one thing: Had any Philadelphia customer recently expanded his orders to include items that could conceivably be used in counterfeiting?

Burns drew a blank. When he returned to Philadelphia, he learned that his men there were drawing blanks, too.

In the printing of money, the currency paper is placed between two pieces of damp muslin just before being put on the press. Burns ordered a canvass of every place in Philadelphia that sold muslin.

The Secret Service operatives uncovered their first promising clue in a dry goods store on Filbert Street. A man, who was not known to any of the clerks, had entered the store not long before the Monroe-head bills had begun to appear, and purchased a bolt of muslin. There had been something furtive about the purchaser. He had been in his late thirties and of nondescript appearance except for one thing—he blinked his eyes constantly.

Burns ordered another canvass of the printing and engraving trade in a search for a man who blinked his eyes constantly. He uncovered no such person. He re-canvassed the supply dealers in New York. Again he came up with nothing.

It now occurred to Burns that the muslin purchaser's eye trouble might have been temporary. In that case, the man might have consulted an eye doctor. Burns and the Secret Service agents questioned eye doctors from morning to night.

The sleuths struck pay dirt of a sort. On a date that coincided with the muslin purchase, a man had gone into the office of an eye specialist on Chestnut Street, just a few blocks from where the muslin had been bought. He had been suffering from a temporary infection, caused by emery dust, that made him blink constantly.

The doctor gave Burns the patient's name and address. The name was fictitious and the address was a vacant lot in Lancaster, a city about an hour west of Philadelphia.

The fact that the blinking man had given the doctor false information about himself was revelatory to Burns. One who is engaged in criminal endeavor covers his tracks at every possible turn.

There was a clue in the fact that the patient's address turned out to be a vacant lot. The man either lived in Lancaster or knew the city well. Otherwise he would not have known the street number of a vacant lot. Burns was disappointed to learn that none of the employees of the Philadelphia printing and engraving plants lived in Lancaster. Printers and engravers doing business in Lancaster itself were quickly screened and eliminated.

Burns was an Irishman. Some Irishmen listen to a source of intelligence known as the little men—invisible creatures who whisper advice in the ear. Burns, too, listened to the little men. He listened to tnem now. They told him to take another crack at the printing and engraving industry, because there he would find the blinking man.

Burns and his agents went to the various establishments in the guise of insurance salesmen selling accident policies. In their sales talks they dwelled particularly on accidents to the eye, which had a high incidence in the engraving field. This enabled them to inquire, without arousing suspicion, if any employees had suffered eye accidents recently.

One of the sleuths called one noon hour at the printing and engraving plant of a firm named Taylor and Bredell, located on the second floor of an industrial building at Ninth and Filbert Streets. The plant was a sizable one and there was plenty of work in the printing and engraving field, yet the Secret Service man found only an office boy on the premises. The young man, who was about fourteen, divulged that his employers— Arthur Taylor and Baldwin Bredell—had laid off all their employees some weeks previously. Taylor and Bredell were, the youth said, conducting experiments of some kind in one room of the establishment. The office boy, whose name was Johnny, said he now had a soft job. He just answered the telephone and the door, and informed all callers that Messrs. Taylor and Bredell were too busy to be disturbed.

"Well," said the Secret Service operative, "I don't suppose Mr. Taylor or Mr. Bredell would be interested in any accident insurance, especially accident insurance covering eye injuries."

"Mr. Taylor might," said the young man. "He got some emery dust in his eyes a while back, and blinked something terrible."

Burns was elated. He felt certain that he was on the trail at last. The Taylor and Bredell plant was in close proximity to both the dry goods store where the muslin had been purchased and the eye doctor who had treated the patient with the fictitious name.

Counterfeiters, however, were the slipperiest of criminals. They must be caught with the actual plates in their possession. If their suspicions were aroused and they disposed of the plates, the evidence to convict would be gone. Burns, knew, therefore, that he would have to proceed with the utmost caution possible.

In order that Taylor and Bredell would not get suspicious about the visit of the so-called insurance salesmen during the noon hour, Burns got in touch with a friend of his—a bona fide salesman—and sent the man to see Taylor. Darned if Taylor didn't buy an accident policy!

Burns rented a room across the street from the building where the Taylor and Bredell plant was located. This enabled him to watch the comings and goings of the two men, although he could not see into their plant.

Taylor and Bredell were both in their late thirties. Each lived in a handsome home in the western part of the city. Certainly, the men, who bore excellent reputations, didn't look like criminals. Burns quietly examined their bank accounts and found, while the men were now handsomely fixed, that each had suffered heavy losses in the stock market more than a year previously. Thus, they could have had a motive—lack of finances—to turn criminal. This was an important step—but only a step.

Suspecting two men, and establishing them as criminals, were totally different matters. Burns took the first step to confirm his suspicion that Taylor was the man who had bought the muslin and given false information to the eye doctor. He had one of his men borrow the camera of a street photographer—one of those fellows who snap pedestrians as they walk along, then hand them cards telling them where to send a quarter for the finished picture. Thus Taylor was snapped on Filbert Street. He didn't accept the card the

41

operative handed him, saying he wasn't interested in a photograph of himself.

The picture turned out fine. It was shown to the eye doctor, and to the clerk in the dry goods store who had sold the muslin to the blinking man. Both identified Taylor.

The next problem was how to get into the engraving plant without being detected. There was a special lock on the entrance door. Burns, from his vantage point in the room across the street, saw that Johnny, the office boy, arrived mornings before Taylor and Bredell. That meant that the young man had a key to the door.

Burns put shadows on Johnny. One day Johnny rushed to a theatre on Chestnut Street during his lunch hour. A Secret Service man learned that he had applied for a job as usher, advertised in the morning papers, but that he was too late.

Burns inserted an ad for an usher. Applicants were instructed to go to a certain hotel suite. Johnny answered the ad. Burns, posing as a theatrical manager, received Johnny in the parlor of the suite. He had purchased an usher's uniform. He told Johnny to go into the bedroom, take off his clothes, and put on the uniform. When Johnny returned to the parlor in the uniform, another agent went through the pockets of the young man's trousers in the bedroom. He removed the key to the engraving company's premises, had a duplicate made by a nearby locksmith who was holding himself in readiness for the job, then returned the key while Burns engaged Johnny in conversation. (P.S. Johnny did not get the job.)

Burns let himself into the Taylor and Bredell premises late that night. He poked around with a flashlight, while agents outside the building maintained a vigil to make certain that neither Taylor nor Bredell surprised him by doing some night work.

At the end of his search, Burns was convinced that Taylor and Bredell were the counterfeiters. No clue led him to this conclusion. Rather, he formed the opinion because of an absence of clues. There was nothing on the premises to indicate that work of any kind was being done, yet Taylor and Bredell were going to their place of business regularly. This indicated to Burns that they were secretly at work on the engraving of a new bill, and they were carrying on their persons the materials they used.

One thing puzzled Burns. He couldn't figure out where the counterfeiters had manufactured their paper. Huge vats and boilers are essential in the manufacture of paper, to mix and boil the pulp. The premises in the building on Filbert Street could accommodate no such equipment.

Burns communed with the little men at this point. The little men told him that pulp was manufactured in Lancaster—the locale of the vacant lot that Taylor had given as his address when consulting the eye doctor.

But where in Lancaster? The Secret Service was getting Taylor and Bredell up in the morning and putting them to bed at night, as constant shadowing is called in crime-detection circles. The two men did nothing of moment. Friends who visited them in their homes were trailed, and eliminated from having any knowledge of the crime. Visitors to their place of business were tabbed, tailed and questioned. The visitors, for the most part, were people who had had previous business dealings with the suspects and who either wanted to buy something from, or sell something to, the printers and engravers. Taylor and Bredell were turning down all work on the grounds that they had a backlog of unfilled orders—an obvious untruth to Burns and further corroboration that the pair were up to no conceivable good.

It occurred to Burns to check the records of the telephone company. Thus he learned that Taylor and Bredell were in the habit of making toll calls to a certain number in Lancaster. The number turned out to be that of a cigar factory operated by two of Lancaster's most prominent citizens—mature men named William Jacobs and W.H. Kendig.

Jacobs and Kendig bore reputations to be prized. Burns wondered why the counterfeiting suspects telephoned their factory frequently. It was of course possible that Taylor and Bredell talked to somebody other than Jacobs and Kendig, once they were connected with the factory. The little men, however, told Burns otherwise.

As luck would have it, the night watchman at the cigar factory fell ill right at the time Burns began to follow the scent in Lancaster. An elderly Secret Service man applied for the job of night watchman—and got it. This enabled Burns to search the cigar factory thoroughly at night to see if he could find some link between the respected manufacturers and the counterfeiting suspects. He found nothing.

Burns decided to examine the books of the company. They were locked in a safe at night. Burns called on a former safecracker who had gone straight—a flesh-and-blood Jimmy Valentine—and this man manipulated the combination by means of sensitive fingers and ears, opened the safe and got the books. He was quick to notice a vitally important fact about the cigar business. Jacobs and Kendig had done a volume of business far in excess of the amount of money they had paid to the United States Government for tobacco tax stamps required to be affixed to every box of the factory's product. The way Burns figured it, Jacobs and Kendig had cheated the Government out of more than fifty thousand dollars during the previous taxable year. They could have done this in only one way—by affixing to their product counterfeit tax stamps.

The picture was now coming into sharp focus for Burns. The respected Jacobs and Kendig, like Taylor and Bredell, had suffered heavy market losses. That had been their motive for resorting to counterfeit tax stamps.

Taylor and Bredell had thus begun their criminal careers by manufacturing spurious revenue stamps for Jacobs and Kendig. They had gone on from there to manufacture money.

The Lancaster cigar factory had the equipment for making currency paper. There was no evidence, however, to the practiced eye of Burns, that any activity relating to counterfeiting had taken place in the factory. Where, then, had such activity taken place?

Jacobs and Kendig owned a warehouse in Lancaster. When Burns went to look over the warehouse, he was flagged down near the structure by two of the agents who had been tailing Taylor and Bredell. The Philadelphia suspects had just entered the place! The denouement was fast approaching.

A careful watch of the warehouse disclosed that it was deserted except for a night watchman and, now, Taylor and Bredell. For several days and nights Burns kept an eye on the place. Taylor and Bredell, careful not to contact Jacobs and Kendig, were staying at a local hotel. They arrived at the warehouse early each morning and remained until early evening, leaving only for lunch at a restaurant nearby.

Burns faced a problem at the warehouse similar to that he had faced when trying to get into Taylor and Bredell's Philadelphia quarters without arousing their suspicion. There was a special lock on the one door of the warehouse. Burns didn't dare to tamper with it. Nor did he dare to try anything like jimmying one of the windows of the place. Caution was needed.

It was August. The baseball season was in full swing. Sandlot games were in progress throughout the land. One such game was being played one day near the warehouse. That gave Burns an idea. He singled out a young man of fourteen—a youth named Lawrence Richie. He sized Richie up as a fellow who could be implicity trusted. He told him that there were criminals at work in the warehouse, enlisted the young man's aid, and coached him for a small but vital role in a real-life detective case.

One noontime, while Taylor and Bredell were out to lunch, Richie batted a baseball through one of the windows of the warehouse. Burns widened the hole in the glass made by the baseball, let himself into the warehouse, and hid, pending the coming of night.

When Taylor and Bredell returned from lunch, they saw young Lawrence Richie standing near the broken window. "Gee," said Richie, skillfully carrying out his part, "I'm awful sorry, but I knocked my ball through your window. My father will pay for the window, and take it out of my allowance, but could I please have my ball back? It's a regular big-league ball, and it must be right inside of where it went through the window."

Taylor and Bredell, with more important things on their minds than a broken window, entered the warehouse, got the ball for young Richie and told him

to never mind having his father pay for a new pane of glass, but to be careful not to repeat what he had done. Richie thanked the men and went away happy. Burn's psychological ruse had completely fooled the suspects.

That night, Burns trailed the night watchman around the darkened warehouse. Finally the watchman fell asleep. Burns then began his search of the place. He came upon two vats filled with mash for making currency paper. He uncovered, too, a cache of counterfeit revenue stamps. He left everything just as it was, and sneaked away before dawn while the watchman was still sleeping. He had learned what he wanted to know.

The trick now was to know just when to strike. If Burns struck prematurely, or too late, his case would be dangerously weakened. There were ways of knowing, however, just from observing Taylor and Bredell, approximately what stage of the game they were in.

Some three weeks after Burns had first discovered the Lancaster warehouse, the suspects left the place one night carrying suitcases. That meant they had completed manufacture of the paper and were taking it into Philadelphia for printing.

In his frequent nocturnal prowls of the Philadelphia premises, Burns noticed a bolt of muslin in a corner of one of the rooms. The muslin would be needed in the final phase of the counterfeiting operation—the dampening of the paper just before it was placed on the press. Up to now, Burns had pretty well made his own circumstances by clever psychological moves. Now luck was with him. On a shelf directly above the muslin was a corkless gallon jug of acid. There were frequent vibrations in the engraving plant from night truck traffic on Filbert Street. What would be more natural than for the vibrations to cause the jug of acid to "walk" to the edge of the shelf and fall on the muslin?

So Burns tipped the acid. It spilled onto the muslin and ruined it. Three days later, agents tailing the suspects noticed Taylor purchasing a bolt of muslin in a dry goods store. Burns knew the hour to strike was drawing near.

The muslin was purchased late in the afternoon. Burns figured the printing process would get under way next day. He was wrong. Taylor and Bredell remained in their plant that night—the first night they had done so since coming under surveillance. Burns figured they were running off the first of the bills while Johnny, the office boy, was not around.

Burns and a group of agents let themselves quietly into the plant. They came upon Taylor and Bredell redhanded. The finest Lincoln-head one-hundred-dollar bill in the entire history of American counterfeiting was just coming off the presses. The most formidable threat to the country's monetary system in the entire history of counterfeiting up to that time was, thanks to months of delicate work, smashed there and then.

Taylor and Bredell went to prison. So did Jacobs and Kendig, whose revenue-stamp crime had been uncovered in the course of the investigation of the more important crime.

Billy Burns, ace sleuth for Uncle Sam, went on to further triumphs. Whatever became of Johnny, the young man who wanted to become an usher, is not recorded. What became of Lawrence Richie, the youth who carried out a small but vital role for the detective, is on record. Richie's contact with Burns, and his brief experience in a crime detective case, decided him to make crime-detection his life work. Eventually, Lawrence Richie became an ace agent of the Secret Service.

The Bus Boy and the Criminals

Tommy Adams, who lived with his parents in the
Greenwich Village district of New York, celebrated his
fifteenth birthday by getting a job as part-time bus boy
in a French restaurant near his home. Tommy's duties
began at five thirty in the afternoon, when he distributed
the napkins, glasses, and silverware to the tables in the
establishment; and carried through dinner, when he
served rolls and butter and filled the water glasses of the
patrons. He worked Monday through Saturday, the
restaurant being closed Sundays.

Tommy was a particularly observant boy. His hobby
was reading character. He used to amuse himself by
trying to figure out what this or that patron did for a

living. Sometimes he learned their actual professions, especially the steady customers, and it often turned out that he had guessed correctly. He was encouraged to pursue his hobby of character reading further.

Late in the winter of the year that Tommy took the job there came to the restaurant a stocky, middle-aged man with furtive manner and darting, shoe-button eyes who struck Tommy as being in a different line from any of the other diners. Tommy couldn't quite figure the man out. The stranger became a steady patron. The more Tommy studied him, the more the man disturbed him. At length the bus boy had the answer—at least, an answer that satisfied him. The man, who spoke English with a decided French accent, was a criminal. Tommy had no proof of his suspicion; he knew in his bones, however, that he was right.

As the weeks passed, and Tommy's suspect continued to frequent the restaurant, he began to have companions. The companions, who seemed also to be French, called the suspect Gabrielle. By April, some two months after he had first appeared, the man called Gabrielle habitually occupied a big round table in the rear of the place where he and his companions could eat and talk in privacy. Gabrielle had four companions in all, and Tommy was convinced that they too, were criminals. One had a scar on his face, another couldn't look Tommy in the eye when Tommy filled his water glass, and the entire group talked in low tones or not at all when Tommy approached their table to serve them.

One particular Saturday night in April, Tommy sensed an air of tenseness and expectancy among the group at the big round table in the rear. It was as if Gabrielle and his four companions were up to something. When Tommy went home that night, he couldn't get the five men out of his mind. The next day he found his mind still wandering to them. What had they been up to?

Monday morning at breakfast, Tommy's father was reading the morning paper. "Here's a terrible thing happened yesterday," he commented. "Five masked men locked a millionaire's whole household in a vault, and got away with two hundred thousand dollars worth of jewelry."

"What a horrible thing to do—lock people in a vault," said Mrs. Adams. "Did the family get out all right?"

"Yes, but no thanks to the robbers. They were left there to die, but one of the servants in the vault used a penknife as a screwdriver to loosen the screws that held the vault lock to the inside of the door. Then he pushed it out and reached through, and turned the outside handle of the vault."

Tommy read the account of the crime when his father had finished with the paper. He filled himself in on additional details. The victims of the crime had been Albert Shattuck, elderly retired financier and philanthropist, his wife, and several servants. The hooded men, waving guns, had descended on the Shattuck home—a three-story mansion on Washington Square North—dur-

ing the quiet of Sunday afternoon. None of the intruders had spoken; they had used threatening gestures rather than words to convey their commands. They had herded everybody down to the cellar, forced them into a huge vault, slammed and locked the door, and left them to suffocate. It had taken the victims more than three hours to get out; another forty-five minutes and they would have died. The New York police called the crime the most heartless on record.

Tommy put the paper down and stared out a window with unseeing eyes. The Shattuck mansion was but a few minutes' walk from the French restaurant where the man called Gabrielle and his four companions had seemed so tense the night before the crime. Tommy was certain—just as certain as he was that he would be late for school if he didn't get going—that the five men he had noticed in the restaurant had committed the most heartless of crimes.

"Dad," he said, "I think I know who engineered that robbery." His father looked incredulous. But incredulity gave way to intense interest and sober belief, as he listened to his son's earnest, alarming story. "You could be right, Tommy," said Mr. Adams. "At least it's my duty as a citizen to report your story to the police."

The police were immediately intrigued. They felt that Tommy had put them on the right trail. After keeping the restaurant under surveillance for several days, they saw no sign of the man called Gabrielle and his four companions. It seemed obvious by now that the quintet had met in the restaurant merely to perfect plans for the crime, then had gone into hiding or fled to distant points once the outrage had been perpetrated.

Tommy spent many hours helping the detectives. He described the man called Gabrielle in great detail, even to the fact that he had a slight bald spot, about the size of a quarter, on the back of his head. There was no doubt in the boy's mind that Gabrielle and his companions had all been French. "How can you be so sure, Tommy?" asked a detective.

Tommy shrugged. "I just know a French accent when I hear one, I suppose. I got used to French accents in the restaurant." The police incorporated Tommy's information into a long cable to the Paris police.

The latter were asked particularly to look through their files for a criminal whose first name was Gabrielle and whose appearance answered Tommy's description of the suspected bandit leader.

Meantime, the police sent circulars throughout the city, state and country, and abroad, describing in detail the stolen fortune in Shattuck gems. There were rings, earrings, pendants, necklaces, and bracelets of rubies, pearls, diamonds, and emeralds—truly a king's ransom.

An answer came from the Paris police. They did not have any idea as to the identities of four of the five men. But they were pretty certain that the leader had been one Gabrielle Mourey; an Apache criminal who had a long record as an evil-doer and who was, at the moment, a fugitive from French justice. A photograph of Gabrielle Mourey was en route, Paris advised.

Tommy Adams sat in police headquarters thumbing through stacks of rogues' gallery pictures. In order not to influence his selection, the police had mixed Gabrielle Mourey's picture with a dozen "muggs" of other criminals. When Tommy came to Mourey's picture, he stopped, opened his eyes a little wider, looked up at the detectives, and said, "This is the man from the restaurant." The fifteen-year-old boy had definitely put the police on the right trail.

When Albert Shattuck and his wife, who had both had such a close call from death, studied the rogues' gallery photos of Gabrielle Mourey, they recognized the criminal as a man who had once worked in their household as a butler under another name. "I could never forget that face," said the financier-philanthropist. "There was something evil in it."

Gabrielle Mourey's face was forthwith incorporated in a police flier that was distributed throughout the United States, Panama, Mexico, Central and South America, and in England and the Continent. The most distinguishing mark on his body, also described, was a tattoo on his right forearm.

The police were not through with Tommy yet. They kept questioning him as to whether he had overheard any bits of conversation between Gabrielle Mourey and

59

his companions, that could be of any value in the manhunt. Tommy could not recall any such conversation. "Keep thinking back, Tommy," urged a detective. "Oftentimes a person hears something and then forgets it, unless he really strains to recall it."

The detective was right. Tommy recalled that one of Mourey's henchmen—the one with the scar on his face—had once said that he had friends in Plaindale, New Jersey. There was no such town as Plaindale in New Jersey, but there was a Plainfield. Detectives went to the New Jersey community and began to watch the patrons of some of the restaurants there.

Early in their search, the detectives spotted a scar-faced man who answered the description of one of the quintet. He was a regular patron at a little French restaurant. But the detectives had to be sure. One night they took Tommy to Plainfield. For several hours Tommy stood on a street corner with a detective. Toward midnight a man came out of the restaurant.

"Here he is, Tommy," whispered the sleuth. "Get a good look at his face when he passes under the street lamp there, and poke me twice if that's him."

Tommy held his breath as the man came closer. Then, when he passed under the street lamp, Tommy got a good look at his face. He poked the detective twice. The detective brought out a handkerchief and blew his nose—a signal to two other detectives nearby to close in on the quarry. The man with the scar was taken

THE BUS BOY AND THE CRIMINALS

without a struggle—thanks, again to fifteen-year-old
Tommy Adams.

The prisoner's name was Moise Bagnoli. He readily
admitted his identity and his participation in the Shattuck crime. He corroborated the police premise that
Gabrielle Mourey had been the leader of the gang.
Mourey had taken half of the loot—one hundred
thousand dollars worth of gems—as his share and
divided the rest among his confederates.

Who, the police wanted to know of the prisoner, were
the other participants in the crime, and where were
they?— And Mourey? Aside from Mourey and Bagnoli,
the others had been Eugene Diaset, Pierre LaMonte
and Paul Camilleri—hardened European criminals all.
Bagnoli had not the slightest idea as to the whereabouts
of Mourey, the leader, and Camilleri, a close friend of
Mourey's, but he knew where Diaset and LaMonte
were. He led the police right to Diaset in a hideout in
New York. The police reached LaMonte's hideout too
late; he had been killed in a quarrel with some other
criminals over the price for a hideout they were selling
him. Bagnoli, the scar-faced one, and Diaset were
quickly convicted and sent to Sing Sing Prison for sixty
years. With two of the bandit quintet in the big house
and one dead, that left two at large—Gabrielle Mourey,
the leader, and his close friend, Paul Camilleri.

Several months had passed since the outrageous
crime had been committed in the house in Washington

Square North. Albert Shattuck, the victim, made a public announcement. He would spend the remaining years of his life and all his millions, if need be, to see that the case was completely solved, meaning the apprehension, conviction and imprisonment of the two remaining fugitives. "I will personally track these men down to the ends of the earth if necessary," said Shattuck. The police admired the retired financier's courage; he was seventy-one years old and in frail health.

The first clue came from San Francisco. There a jeweler bought two ruby rings from a dark, stocky stranger, later to discover that they were part of the Shattuck loot. The stranger had lived at a small hotel near the jewelry shop, but when the jeweler notified the police, the man had checked out of the hotel.

Shattuck took the first train for San Francisco on receipt of the information. He went to the hotel where the suspect had stayed. He questioned bellboys and other employees about the man. Shattuck emerged with one clue: the suspect had been looking at travel folders on Mexico when a waiter had gone to his room with breakfast one morning just before his departure. Shattuck knew the suspect had been Mourey. He had had a small bald spot, about the size of a quarter, on the back of his head—a clue first given to the police by observant Tommy Adams.

Shattuck now went to Mexico. The Federal police there had just run down a clue in a small town twenty miles from Mexico City. A man reported to look like the fugitive Mourey had visited the town and given someone a handsome piece of jewelry as a present. The jewelry turned out to be part of the Shattuck loot. But by the time the police reached the town, the quarry had disappeared.

Shattuck traveled throughout Mexico, sometimes going into the mountains alone on horseback in search of his quarry. The aged man underwent trying rigors of various kinds, but his spirit carried him through.

The hunter was in Mexico when the quarry turned up in Panama. There a man with very dark skin went into a physician's office and asked that a tattoo mark be removed from his right forearm. The tattoo was the one mentioned on the police flier describing Mourey, but the physician had not seen the flier and didn't know this man was wanted by the police. The doctor told the patient that the removal of the tattoo would be very painful and suggested anesthetic. The patient was against an anesthetic. He insisted that the removal be done without one. He could, he said, stand the pain.

During the operation, the man fainted from the pain. By way of reviving him, the doctor loosened his collar and shirt. When he did so, he noticed that his patient's chest and neck were several shades whiter than his face. Here, then, was a man who had darkened his skin as disguise. Why? The doctor went into another room and reported the suspicious patient to the police. When he returned to his operating room, the man had revived and disappeared. The police showed the doctor a flier of Mourey: the French criminal had been the patient.

Shattuck went to Panama. There he organized expeditions into the jungles of the Isthmus, seeking the fugitive's hideout. While Shattuck was on one such expedition, Mourey turned up in Rio de Janiero. There the story was similar to that of San Francisco; the man had sold some of the Shattuck gems to local jewelers, only to have them discover the true source after he had vanished from his hotel.

In Rio, Shattuck, standing up miraculously under the rigors of the chase, questioned employees of the hotel where Mourey had stayed. The man had fallen into conversation with a chambermaid about the Philippines. The maid had once worked in a hotel in Manila, and Mourey had asked her all manner of questions about the country.

On the strength of the information from the chambermaid in Rio, Shattuck went to Manila. When he reached that city, he went to the police with the information he had picked up in Rio. The police had news for him—the most disheartening sort of news. Mourey had been in Manila. But it was the same story all over again. He had sold some gems, the gems had been recognized as Shattuck loot, but Mourey had gone by the time the police could act.

Albert Shattuck returned to New York. A year had passed now since the quiet Sunday afternoon when he and his wife and servants had been entombed. He knew he could not have very much longer to live. He was not well. His body was weakening, but his spirit was as strong as ever. He rededicated himself to catching the two fiends at large. He booked passage on a round-the-world cruise ship. He had a strange hunch that somewhere, along the route of the liner, he would spot one or both of the remaining criminals.

In every port at which the liner docked as it traveled westward around the globe—Honolulu, Yokohama, Hong Kong—Albert Shattuck got off and roamed the main street, the side streets, and the alleys, searching, searching. Death, he knew, was coming closer; the criminals seemed to be as far away as ever. Then one day as the ship was going slowly westward through the Suez Canal at Port Said, the toughest city in the world, and Albert Shattuck was leaning on the rail, looking at the laborers on the edge of the canal, he spotted a familiar face—the face of Gabrielle Mourey. His long hunt was almost at an end. Mourey, in laborer's garb, was scanning the faces of the passengers. His gaze and the gaze of Albert Shattuck locked. But the ship was in motion, on its way from Port Said. Gabrielle Mourey began to run. "Stop that man! Stop this ship! Stop this ship." The crew and the other passengers looked at the old man as if he had suddenly gone out of his mind. The ship did not stop. Neither did the running man on the shore. The distance between the ship and the running man grew greater. Soon the man was out of sight. Presently, courageous old Albert Shattuck sank into a deck chair and burst into tears.

Back in New York, a strange happening came to pass. Tommy Adams, the youth who had originally put the police on the trail, suddenly recalled something, a bit of information dredged up from the recesses of his subconscious after more than a year. He recalled he had once heard Mourey saying that there was no place in the world like Paris in June. This was June. Tommy turned the scrap of information over to the New York police. The latter had been apprised of the episode at Port Said. The police in the Suez port had gone to work trailing Gabrielle Mourey. The fugitive's path was picked up here, lost there, picked up again, lost again, in several European countries. But the trail pointed to the general direction of Paris—and this was June!

Gabrielle Mourey and his confederate Paul Camilleri were known to prefer Apache joints when in the French capital. Albert Shattuck, kept abreast of developments by wireless to his ship, disembarked from the ship at Marseilles. He took a train to Paris. There he came to the end of his long trail.

He reached the capital just in time to be greeted by the news that the French police had picked up both

Gabrielle Mourey and Paul Camilleri. Albert Shattuck sat in a French courtroom and heard Mourey and Camilleri sentenced to life on that fortress of the condemned—Devil's Island. Mr. Shattuck lived long enough to return to the United States and reward Tommy Adams, the lad who played such a vital role in one of the most unusual manhunts of modern times.

The Cub Reporter Cracks a Case!

One steaming mid-summer day the hard-boiled city editor of a Topeka newspaper beckoned to the sheet's cub reporter—a young man of eighteen named Richard Alden Swallow. "Dick," said the city editor, "take a run out to Maple Hill and look into this."

The editor handed Swallow a letter bearing the postmark of a hamlet in the Kansas prairies. It was from a farm couple named Welch, whose eighteen-year-old son, John, had vanished. The parents feared that their son had been murdered.

Dick Swallow's pulse quickened. He had dreamed of solving a big front-page murder mystery and making a name for himself in the fourth estate. The trouble was that he had been assigned only to such unexciting happenings as Sunday school picnics and meetings of garden clubs. Here, at last, was his big chance.

Swallow thanked his boss for the opportunity. "Probably nothing to it, Dick," said the city editor. "That young man probably ran away because he didn't like life on a farm in the prairies. Can't say I blame him."

Maple Hill, a map dot of a few hundred souls, shimmered in the August heat when Dick Swallow stepped off the afternoon train. The main street was a dirt road that ran between unpainted frame houses and a sprinkling of stores. On all sides the prairies stretched to the horizon, as empty-seeming as the wide, cloudless sky above it. Here indeed was a veritable no-man's-land.

The parents of the missing John Welch lived five miles from town. The sole means of transportation was in a rig owned by the town's livery-man—Rufus King.

Swallow had an uneasy feeling, as he sat alongside the livery man during the ride. King was a big brute of a man in his early fifties. He was dark, unkempt to a disgusting degree, and, Swallow thought, somehow sinister.

During the ride, King said to Swallow, "You're a reporter, ain't you?"

Swallow nodded, and asked the man how he knew.

King grunted. "The Welches write to all the papers in Kansas. They think Johnnie was murdered—and that I murdered him!

"Johnnie worked for me. He was my helper. He slept on a cot in the stable. He used to go home to his folks weekends. One weekend last January he didn't go home, but just disappeared."

"But why," pressed Swallow, "would Johnnie's parents think you murdered him?"

King laughed hoarsely. He tapped his forehead with his forefinger. "They're not right up here."

Swallow found the Welches quiet, intelligent people —quite a contrast to the way King had pictured them. They were deeply sincere in their belief that Rufus King had murdered their son. But they had only suspicion, not proof.

"Where," Swallow asked, "would Mr. King have disposed of the body, assuming he killed your son?"

"Rufus King," said the missing young man's father, "is not only a liveryman. He is also the town's undertaker, and he's used to digging graves too."

What, Swallow asked, would King's motive have been? "Money. Johnnie had saved up more than a hundred dollars. He carried it with him all the time, in a money belt."

Back in the city room of his paper, Swallow reported to his boss. He wanted to write a story about the suspicions of the Welches. "King," he said, "is a bad man. Something tells me the Welches are right about him."

"Dick, if you ever wrote such a story, King could sue the paper for everything it's worth. You can't accuse a man of murder without proof."

So Dick Swallow went back to the routine drudgery that is heaped on a newspaper cub and was so busy he hardly had time to think of his suspect out in the Kansas prairies. Then, in August a year later, another letter came into the paper. This one was from a man in Nebraska named Ringer. His brother—William Ringer, a hunchback itinerant peddler of cheap jewelry—had vanished the previous December, after having spent some time in Wabaunsee County, Kansas. The peddler, his brother said, usually carried considerable cash on his person.

Once again Swallow's pulse quickened. Maple Hill, the hamlet where King lived, was in Wabaunsee County. And so, a year almost to the day after he had first gone to Maple Hill to look into the disappearance of John Welch, Dick Swallow set foot in the hamlet for the second time.

The reporter went straight to Rufus King's stable. King, sitting at a desk near a horse stall, eyed him suspiciously, splattered the wall with tobacco juice, then roared, "You here again! What do you want this time?"

Swallow showed King the letter from Nebraska. King looked off into space, then said, "Sure, I remember that old hunchback. Fact is, I drove him around when he was peddlin' his stuff here last Christmas time."

"Where did he go, do you know, Mr. King?"

King shrugged. "That I wouldn't know. All I know is I drove him to the railroad depot a couple of days after Christmas and he caught the night train for Topeka."

King was so straightforward and disarming that the reporter told himself he had suspected the man without good reason. He thanked King and returned to his paper.

Another year passed. And a third letter came to Swallow's paper. A man named Willard, who lived in Ohio, wrote in to ask if the paper would find out anything about the whereabouts of his parents—Mr. and Mrs. John Willard. The Willards had been elderly folks who had gone to Wabaunsee County, Kansas, the previous spring, to look around for a home in which to spend their remaining years, only to vanish like two figures rubbed from a blackboard. "I am sure," wrote the man from Ohio, "that something terrible has happened to my father and mother."

For the third time in as many summers, Dick Swallow landed in Maple Hill to look into a disappearance. As he got off the train, a summer storm was coming up over the Kansas prairies. It was mid-afternoon but the hamlet was plunged into night-like darkness. Hanging signs on the few stores on the main street creaked and banged in the high wind. Electric lights winked on, looking weird in the unnatural dimness.

This, Dick Swallow told himself, was a hamlet accursed. He had learned, since his last visit, of Maple Hill's affinity for disaster. It had once been the scene of a train wreck in which more than thirty lives were lost. A few years previously, it had been all but wiped out by a fire of mysterious origin. Still later, it had been seriously decimated by an epidemic. And now, Dick Swallow knew in his bones, as he started up the gloomy main street, Maple Hill was the lair of a modern bluebeard.

Rufus King glowered at the young man. "I suppose," he roared, "you think I killed somebody else now!" King broke into a laugh—a grim laugh that chilled Swallow.

"I'm trying to locate people named Willard—Mr. and Mrs. John Willard," said the reporter.

"Elderly folks?" asked King.

"Yes. They were in this section last spring, looking for a place to live."

"I remember them," said King. He was disarming again. "Drove them out to a boarding house in Rossville. That's a few miles from here."

Swallow went to the boarding house. The people who ran it distinctly recalled the Willards. They had become very friendly with the Ohio couple when the Willards had boarded with them while hunting for a place in which to settle down.

"What happened to them?" asked Swallow.

"We don't know," said the boarding house mistress. "They left here to go to another part of the state to look at property. They promised to write us, but never did. That didn't seem like them—not to keep their word."

"Who drove them to the railroad station?"

"That liveryman over in the Maple Hill. I think his name is King."

"Did Mr. and Mrs. Willard carry any valuables on them?"

"I believe they carried quite some cash."

Swallow found a real estate man who said that the Willards had looked at some land owned by a man named John Turnbull—the village blacksmith of Maple Hill. Swallow sought out Turnbull. The smithy was a great brawny man, like the smithy in the Longfellow poem—elderly and with a long, white beard.

Old John, as Turnbull was known, was definitely hostile to Swallow. "My advice to you, young man," he said, "is to go away and forget all about the Willards. Nothing happened to them. They went away, that's all."

Swallow wasn't so easily put off. "Are you friendly with Rufus King?" he asked the blacksmith.

Turnbull stiffened. "Rufus King is one of the finest men ever to draw the breath of life!" Turnbull moved menacingly toward Swallow. "Now get out of here," he roared, "and never come back!"

The seat of Wabaunsee County—Alma—was some fifteen miles away. Swallow went there and sought out the Sheriff—a man whose qualifications for his official job were something less than they might have been.

Swallow told the Sheriff that he suspected that Maple Hill had become a port of missing men. First John Welch had vanished. Then Ringer, the peddler, had disappeared. And now the Willards might just as well have stepped through a hole into space.

"Mr. Swallow," said the Sheriff, "let me tell you something: The parents of John Welch came to see me when he dropped from sight. They said Rufe King killed him. Fact of the matter is the parents mistreated Johnnie. That's why he run away."

"How do you know that, sir?" asked Swallow.

"Johnnie wrote a letter to some friends right in Alma. The letter was from Texas. I seen it with my own eyes."

"But what about the others, Sheriff—the hunchback peddler and the Willards?"

"I don't know about the Willards, but from what you say they went away, that's all. Just because people don't write a lot of letters after they leave don't mean they're murdered. As for that old peddler, I know for a fact he was alive after he left here. He left a sweater with some people he boarded with over in the next town, and he wrote and had them send it to him couple of months after he left."

"And you saw that letter, too, Sheriff?" asked Swallow.

" 'Deed I did. I looked into things when the peddler's kinfolk wrote and asked me to locate him."

Swallow returned to Topeka, the routine of the city room and reluctantly forgot his dream of a big front-page murder story. Other reporters on the sheet began to kid him about his exploits in Maple Hill. "What's the matter, Sherlock," asked one. "Did the big mystery blow up right in your face?"

Swallow grinned and kept his own counsel. A good reporter, like a good detective, has an instinct that tells him when to keep going in the face of obstacles. And Dick Swallow was a good reporter. It made no difference to him that the Sheriff had seen letters from John Welch and Ringer, the peddler. Something inside him assured him that Welch and Ringer, along with the Willards, were murdered, and that Rufus King was the murderer.

On his days off, Swallow journeyed to Maple Hill, at his own expense, and snooped around. He made it a point to keep out of sight of Rufus King. By making a cautious inquiry here and there, Swallow learned that King had, during the first world war, worked as a teamster on a government construction job in Chanute, Kansas.

Swallow hastened to Chanute. Since years had passed since King had worked in Chanute, finding someone who had known him took a little doing. But

Swallow finally located another man who remembered King. It was from this man that the reporter obtained the following story:

King and another teamster named Ike Manning had become very friendly. Manning was a great fisherman. King took up fishing, too. The two men went fishing together one day. Only King returned. There had been an accident, King reported, and poor Manning had drowned. Manning was known to carry large sums of money on his person. When his body was recovered, no money was found on him.

Swallow returned to Wabaunsee County. There in the courthouse at Alma, he dug into the records of missing persons. A Mexican laborer who had lived near the county seat had mysteriously vanished some five years previously. The report on the case disclosed, among other things, that the Mexican had worked from time to time at Rufus King's livery stable!

Swallow returned to Topeka, hot on the scent now, and laid his suspicions before an assistant on the staff of the Attorney General of the state of Kansas. "Evidence," demanded the state official. "We need evidence to go on. We can't proceed on suspicion alone. Everything you have learned, Mr. Swallow, could very well be coincidence."

"But," protested the reporter, "there is a pattern that all these disappearances fall into. Everyone who disappeared was last seen with Rufus King, and everyone who disappeared carried money."

"But the letters that the Sheriff saw—the letters about John Welch and the hunchback peddler—they were real enough."

"They could have been fakes," countered Swallow. "Fakes written by Rufus King himself and given to someone to mail from distant points."

The Attorney General's Office refused to move.

Swallow went back to Maple Hill. He confronted Old John Turnbull, the blacksmith, again. "You look like a kindly man," said Swallow. "There must be some powerful reason why you treated me as you did last time I called on you."

Old John Turnbull stood at his forge, looking at the young man. "I don't have long to live," he said at length. "I might as well talk to you."

The story that Old John Turnbull had to tell was as simple as it was terrifying. He, like many others in Maple Hill, lived in mortal dread of Rufus King. He and others subscribed to the theory of John Welch's parents—that King was a murderer.

"There were two or three young men who helped King around the stable before Johnnie Welch," Turnbull told Swallow. "They dropped from sight, too."

"What do you think King did with the bodies, Mr. Turnbull?"

"I've often seen him digging and puttering around in an old shed back of his stable. Wouldn't be a bit surprised if he's hid something there."

Swallow took up a vigil behind King's livery stable.

One day, when the suspect appeared in his funeral clothes and drove off on his hearse, the reporter went to work. He examined the earth in and around the shed that Old John Turnbull had spoken about. He found one soft spot. He got a shovel from the stable and dug into the soft spot. He came upon two things not far below the surface—a man's hat and a lady's dress.

Instinct told Swallow that he had only scratched the surface. But King would be back soon. He didn't want to arouse his suspicions. He filled in the earth, stamped it down so that it would not give the appearance of having been disturbed, replaced the shovel and went to Topeka with the hat and the dress.

Swallow sent the two articles of apparel to the son of the missing Willards. The son promptly identified the dress as belonging to his mother, but said the hat was too small to have fitted his father. Swallow now sent the hat to Nebraska—to the brother of Ringer, the missing peddler. The brother telegraphed back that the hat was positively that of the vanished hunchback.

In the face of such evidence, the Attorney General agreed to act. Rufus King, with the instinct of an animal that knows when danger threatens, had vanished when investigators of the Attorney General's office, accompanied by Dick Swallow, reached Maple Mill.

Dick Swallow devoted his deductive powers to the whereabouts of Rufus King while the Attorney General's investigators dug up the grounds behind the livery stable. The remains of nine persons were unearthed. The hunchback peddler was identified by the deformities in his bone structure. John Welch and the Willards were identified by dental work.

Swallow learned from the railroad station agent in Maple Hill that Rufus King had bought a ticket to Topeka. In Topeka, a railroad ticket seller studied a photograph of Rufus King that Swallow had obtained from the home from which the liveryman-undertaker had so hastily departed. The ticket seller clearly recalled the man as the purchaser of a ticket to Pueblo, Colorado.

On the basis of Swallow's information, the Attorney General's office wired a description of King to the police of Pueblo. King was picked up in short order and returned to Kansas. Convicted of murder, he was sentenced to spend the rest of his natural life behind the walls of the Kansas State Penitentiary.

Richard Alden Swallow, now turned twenty-one, was made a full-fledged reporter because of his remarkable work in detecting and getting the evidence of a bluebeard who had covered his tracks so well that he had not even been suspected over the years. A brilliant career in newspaper work had but begun.

Paper Bag Bandit

Kenneth Layne, at the age of thirteen, had been a Scout for several years. Scouting had taught him, among other things, the importance of developing his powers of observation. Ken had a paper route which he took care of every day after school. It was while on his route, which he covered by bicycle, that he practiced the art of observing things. He noticed when there were new curtains in the windows of the home of one of his customers; he observed what kinds of vegetables and flowers were in the gardens on his route; he was quick to notice when new people moved into a neighborhood and old people moved away. It was Kenneth Layne's highly-developed powers of observation that were one day to come to the aid of the police of his city, a community of medium size within one hundred miles of New York City.

One afternoon, late in April, 1949, the headline across the top of the *Evening Express*, the paper Ken delivered, was devoted to the appearance in town of a bandit with a new technique. The brigand in question had appeared in the department store of Sternberg & Son, carrying a paper bag. He had made his way to the rear of the store, to the cashier's department, arousing no suspicion. Then he opened the paper bag, withdrew a blue-steel automatic, and announced, "This is a stickup! Everybody keep quiet and nobody gets hurt. Now hand over the money." The bandit had made off with almost fifteen hundred dollars in bills and silver coins, jumped into a car standing at the curb, and made a clean getaway. Eye-witnesses described the getaway car as a 1948 black Dodge sedan, but nobody had obtained the license number.

Ken Layne, like many young men his age, was an automobile fan. He knew every detail of the various models almost as soon as they came off the assembly lines. He knew the make and year and model of cars in practically every garage along his paper route. There were several 1948 Dodge sedans, the model the bandit had used.

One such car belonged to a new out-of-town couple who had just rented a furnished house in the two-hundred block on Newell Street—Mr. and Mrs. Walter DeKalb. The DeKalbs were a couple in their late twenties; Mrs. DeKalb wore a lot of jewelry and gave off an aura of strong perfume, such as an actress might be expected to wear; Mr. DeKalb was a dark, slick-haired man, whose plain black necktie was always tied in a small, tight knot and who wore natty dark blue suits and shoes shined so highly that you could practically see your face in them. The DeKalbs were great newspaper readers; they took not only the *Evening Express* from Ken, but *The New York Times* and the *Daily News* as well—the only customers on the entire route who took New York papers.

The "paper bag" bandit, as the *Evening Express* had started to call the man who had held up Sternberg & Son, had covered his tracks well. The police were frank to admit they hadn't the slightest idea who he was or where he had come from or gone. Nobody in the department store had recognized him nor could anybody there recollect ever having seen him before. He was described as a natty dresser, dark-complexioned, and about thirty years of age.

Ken, reading the description of the paper bag bandit in the *Evening Express*, noted that it fitted, in a very general way, the description of his new customer, Mr.

85

Walter DeKalb. Then he caught himself up short. What right had he to make even a mental connection between Mr. DeKalb and the paper bag bandit just because Mr. DeKalb was dark-complexioned, about thirty, was a natty dresser, and owned a 1948 black Dodge sedan? Similar descriptions could fit hundreds of people.

Early in May the paper bag bandit put in his second appearance. This time, carrying his paper bag again, he walked into the offices of the Monroe County Building and Loan Association, on the second floor of the Macy Building, in the downtown district, during the noon hour. Only two clerks—young ladies—were on duty. The bandit opened his bag, brought out his gun, and quietly requested the young ladies to hand over all the cash on the premises. He walked out with almost six hundred dollars.

The bandit had to go down a flight of stairs before he reached the street. By the time he did reach the street, one of the young ladies had leaned out a window of the building-and-loan premises, and yelled to passersby. She saw the bandit when he appeared from the building corridor leading to the street. "That's him!" she screamed. The man ducked back into the building and apparently raced through a passageway that led to an exit at a service entrance, because two men who started in somewhat tardy pursuit found no trace of him.

As he read the details of the second holdup in the *Evening Express,* Ken noted that the young ladies described the bandit as having worn a blue suit, highly polished shoes and a tightly knotted black necktie. Moreover, the bandit had had an engaging smile. He had upon entering the building-and-loan association offices carrying his paper bag, looked around, as if in quest of information, and when one of the girls approached him, he had smiled—a quick, ready smile, displaying teeth that the young lady described to an *Evening Express* reporter as resembling a smile in a dentifrice advertisement.

Ken fell to thinking about that quick smile and those perfect teeth. Mr. DeKalb, his new customer, had such a smile and such teeth. He dressed the way the bandit had dressed, too. That night at dinner, Ken mentioned to his father and mother the fact that one of his new customers fitted, in a general way, the description of the paper bag bandit. Ken's dad happened to be a lawyer. Mr. Layne finished his coffee and studied his son. "Ken," he said, "there are many cases on record of circumstances indicating things that just are not so. Even if you told me a good deal more about this—what is his name, Mr. DeKalb?—I would still not be convinced that there is the slightest connection between him and this so-called paper bag bandit. A person must be very, very careful before pointing the finger of suspicion at anyone."

Three nights after the building-and-loan holdup, the paper bag bandit put in his third appearance. This time, he drew into a filling station on the edge of the city, and asked the man who ran the place to fill up his gas tank. While the proprietor was at the pump the bandit alighted from his car—the 1948 black Dodge sedan—as if to stretch his legs. He carried a paper bag. The filling-station proprietor looked at the customer as he reached into the bag, but thought he was reaching for a sandwich, as tourists often did.

Then he saw the blue-steel automatic. The bandit got ninety-odd dollars from the cash register, hopped into the car and was off. The filling-station proprietor got the license number of the black Dodge—a license tag that had been issued a third of the way across the country, in the state of Michigan.

The local police wired the Michigan authorities, requesting details about the person to whom the license had been issued. Back came the reply that the plates had been issued to Albert Fox, who was, at the moment, a fugitive from the state of Michigan where he was wanted for armed robbery. The Michigan authorities forwarded a rogues' gallery picture of Fox. It was published in the *Evening Express.*

If Ken Layne had been suspicious of his customer, Mr. DeKalb, his suspicions were now somewhat allayed. In the first place, Mr. DeKalb did not have Michigan plates on his Dodge, but plates of the state

89

where he was residing. Moreover, he bore but a slight resemblance to the rogues' gallery picture published in the *Evening Express*. The fugitive Fox wore eyeglasses, had a small moustache, and parted his hair on the side. There were, as there usually are in such cases, conflicting descriptions of the paper bag bandit. Some eyewitnesses, who had seen the man, identified him as Fox; others said he had been clean-shaven and had not worn eyeglasses.

May dropped from the calendar, and June, and Ken found himself on his summer vacation from school. In addition to his paper route, he got a part-time job in a downtown sporting goods store, working mornings, both in the package-and-delivery department and as a junior salesman. Then something happened that lends support to the adage that truth is stranger than fiction. Next door to the sporting goods store was Orton the Optician. Ken happened to be going out of the store one day early in July when whom should he see going into Orton's but Mr. DeKalb, his paper-route customer. Mr. DeKalb nodded pleasantly to Ken, and flashed that quick smile he had.

Ken wondered what Mr. DeKalb might be doing in Orton's. He didn't wear glasses, nor did Mrs. DeKalb. Could it be that Mr. DeKalb was being fitted for glasses? A week or so later, Ken saw Mr. DeKalb going into the optician's again. He grew more curious—but not nearly so curious as when he saw him making a third visit to Orton's. Why all these visits? Mr. DeKalb wasn't wearing glasses, so he couldn't have gone to Orton's for glasses. But could he? Could he have been fitted for contact lenses—the kind of lenses that fit right over the eyeball and that can't be noticed even by a person standing a few feet away?

While Ken was wondering about the reason for Mr. DeKalb's visits to the optician's, the paper bag bandit struck for the fourth time in as many months. This latest depredation was the Security Bank & Trust Company. He walked in, during the noon hour when the clerical staff was at skeleton force, carrying the paper bag. He took the blue-steel automatic out of the bag in front of a receiving teller's window, leveled the weapon at the teller, and commanded the teller to shove a stack of ten-dollar bills through the wicket. The alarm in front of the bank, set off when the teller stepped on a foot button, began to clang just as the bandit was running from the institution. He darted into a passageway between the bank and another building, before pursuit could be organized, made his way to a parking lot, got into his black Dodge and was off. The Dodge was again carrying the Michigan license tags that had been noted on the occasion of the previous hold-up. The paper bag bandit's take at the bank was more than twelve hundred dollars.

Ken read and re-read the stories in the *Evening Express* about the search for the bandit. Chief of Police

Wood Humphries expressed the opinion that the paper bag bandit might be living right in town, under an alias, and posing as a respectable citizen. Ken began to wonder about Mr. DeKalb all over again. His mind went back to those eye-witness stories that the bandit had been clean-shaven and had not worn eyeglasses. He began to wonder, too, just what Mr. DeKalb did for a living. He had often seen the man sitting on the front porch of his home when the papers were delivered. Ken usually hit the DeKalb home a few minutes after 4:00 P.M.—rather early for a man to be home from work.

Ken had friends all along his paper route, some of them Scouts. One lived directly across the street from the DeKalb's. Ken asked him what Mr. DeKalb did for a living. "Search me, Ken," said the youth. "My dad was wonderin' the same thing. Mr. DeKalb claims he's a salesman, or something, but Dad says he don't see how he sells anything staying home all the time."

Ken's next move was to ask a question of a young man who ran errands for Orton the Optician. Did he know why Mr. DeKalb had visited the optician's several times? The DeKalb account was looked up. Mr. DeKalb had had a prescription refilled—a prescription for a contact lens for the right eye. The prescription, according to the Orton records, had originally been issued in the state of Michigan—the state where the license tags for the bandit car had been issued. Mr. DeKalb had damaged one of his contact lenses, come into Orton's and had another one made.

Ken was more suspicious of Mr. DeKalb than he had ever been. The contact lenses explained a lot. They could explain the absence of eyeglasses, which Albert Fox, the Michigan fugitive, had worn. If Mr. DeKalb were really Albert Fox, he could have shaved off his moustache and parted his hair a different way. The fact that Mr. DeKalb spent most of his time around the house was at least not incompatible with the theory of Chief of Police Humphries that Fox, the criminal, could very well be posing as a respectable citizen and living right in the city. But how to explain the Michigan plates? Ken knew the DeKalb plates; he even knew the numbers on them.

It was in August, four months after he had first appeared, that the paper bag bandit committed his fifth crime. This time he stuck up another filling station, again on the outskirts of the city. During his getaway he scraped the right front fender of the black Dodge with the Michigan license tags. The damage to the bandit's car was slight; the fender, according to the attendant at the filling station who saw it graze one of the pumps, probably hadn't even been dented. It had barely touched the pump, but it had touched it enough to leave traces of black paint.

This fifth crime was committed during the forenoon, so that a full account of it appeared in the *Evening*

Express. Ken read every detail before starting out on his route. Mr. DeKalb was sitting on the front porch a few minutes after four when Ken cycled into the street. Mr. DeKalb's black Dodge sedan, with its local license tags, was parked in front of the house. Ken approached the car from the rear, traveling the same direction as the Dodge faced, so that it wasn't possible for him to see the right fender as he passed.

Ken thought quickly. Instead of throwing Mr. DeKalb's papers up on the porch, he alighted from his bicycle and delivered them to Mr. DeKalb by hand. As an excuse for so doing, he said, "I just wanted to ask you if the deliveries are satisfactory, sir, and if there is any other service I can give you." Mr. DeKalb, who seemed a trifle nervous, smiled and thanked Ken and said there wasn't anything more he could think of. As Ken walked down off the porch he got a good look at the right front fender of the Dodge. Sure enough, it was scratched.

That night, Ken reported everything to his dad: the scratched fender, the contact lens originally prescribed in Michigan, the fact that Mr. DeKalb never seemed to work—all the suspicious circumstances. This time his father was grave. He walked to the telephone and called Chief of Police Humphries.

Next afternoon the *Evening Express* carried a photograph of one of its carriers—Kenneth Layne—on the front page. Ken was the city's hero. His powers of observation, originally developed as a result of Scouting, had solved the mystery of the paper bag bandit.

Walter DeKalb, the apparently respectable citizen, and Albert Fox, the Michigan fugitive, in truth, were one and the same. Fox, alias DeKalb, had chosen to ignore the scratches. Criminally bold, he had made it a point to park his Dodge out in front of his house, for everybody to see, secure in the knowledge that the police were searching for a scratched fender on a Dodge with Michigan tags. Fox, alias DeKalb, had been clever—but not clever enough for the observant Kenneth Layne.

Martin Polk and the Counterfeit Money

M artin Polk, a young man of seventeen who lives in a congested district on the upper West Side of New York City, would be the first to affirm the old adage that truth is stranger than fiction and that it is, moreover, fraught with coincidence. Martin makes his home with his mother and his younger brother, Bill, Jr., in a small apartment in a housing development. Martin, who lost his dad in World War II, is, although still a high school student, usually referred to by his mother as the head of the household. He works in a neighborhood department store after school and Saturdays. His pay, coupled with what his mother earns as a file clerk for a large insurance company, and gets from a government pension, is contributed to the household expenses and savings for the future education of Martin and Bill.

Mrs. Polk and Martin and Bill are a happy trio, moving in a peaceful orbit that finds days filled with work and accomplishment, nights occupied by pleasant relaxation such as movies, radio programs and reading, and hikes and Sunday picnics in the good weather. Altogether, Mrs. Polk and her two sons are hardly the kind of people who might expect to find themselves drawn into the machinations of a dangerous, hunted criminal. Yet that is precisely what happened just two years ago.

It all began one pleasant afternoon in May, when a quiet-mannered man, dressed in a dark suit, walked into the department store where Martin worked and asked to see Mr. Simmons, the manager. It so happened that Mr. Simmons was standing right near Martin's counter in the men's wear department when the stranger appeared. The man reached into his pocket, drew out a paper of some kind, and held a low-voiced conversation with Mr. Simmons. Then he handed the manager several more papers and walked from the store.

Mr. Simmons studied the papers for a moment, then looked up. His gaze caught Martin's. "Here, Martin," he said, handing Martin one of the papers, "I'm to pass these out to all our employees. I might as well start with you. That was a Special Agent of the Secret Service who was just in here."

What Martin found himself reading was a circular put out by the United States Secret Service. The paper described in detail a new and dangerous counterfeit five-dollar bill that had been appearing in various sections of New York City for some months now. The counterfeit, said the circular, was one of the cleverest and, therefore, one of the most dangerous that the Secret Service had encountered in some years. The bill was, in fact, practically perfect except for one detail: the portrait of Abraham Lincoln, which normally shows more of the right side of the martyred President's face than the left, had been transposed, so that more of the left side than the right side appeared—something that the average person simply did not notice.

As a matter of fact, the counterfeits so resembled real money that some of them had not only been accepted by cashiers of stores, theaters and other commercial establishments, but had actually been accepted by some busy bank tellers when the bills had gone to the banks for deposit.

"There's no telling," said Martin's boss, the head of the men's wear department, "when this counterfeiter might come in here. Just keep a sharp eye out for a face of Lincoln that is looking the wrong way. Once you see that, you can check on the serial number of the bill, and the rest of the details."

Martin carried the Secret Service circular with him at all times. He, of course, carefully scrutinized every five-dollar bill that was tendered to him. He didn't see anything that looked like the counterfeit. It wasn't until one Sunday morning in June, about a month after the Special Agent had come into the department store, that Martin Polk walked right into a situation that was a little stranger than fiction. Mrs. Polk and her two sons were about to leave for church when Mrs. Polk said, "Oh, my, I almost forgot my pocketbook; then I wouldn't have had money for the collection!"

Young Bill grinned and reached into his pocket. "Don't worry, Mother," he said, "I have money." He held out a funny-looking bill.

"You and your play money," said Mrs. Polk with a smile.

Martin examined the bill. It was bright green—too green to give a semblance of reality. The serial numeral and certain other details were smudged, and it was printed only on one side of a piece of ordinary white paper, the other side being blank. But there were two things about the bill that arrested Martin's attention. One was that it bore a picture of Abraham Lincoln, and play money does not bear pictures of Presidents (too close a copy of genuine currency is violation of the law). Secondly, this picture of Lincoln was facing the wrong way—just the way the picture in the counterfeit faced. Martin asked Bill where he had obtained the bill. His younger brother shrugged. "From some kid they call Red," said Bill. "He sells it."

Martin stuck the bill in his pocket, telling Bill he would give him another one in exchange for it later, and said nothing more. But all during the church services his mind was on that piece of funny-looking money.

Immediately after dinner that afternoon, Martin, without a word to anyone, hurried over to the precinct police station. He showed the bill to the Lieutenant who laughed. "This is no counterfeit," he said. "Nobody would ever expect to pass a thing like this." Then Martin reached into his pocket and showed the Lieutenant the circular that the Special Agent of the Secret Service had left at the department store. The Lieutenant studied the circular, then the funny-looking bill. "Say, young man," he said to Martin, "maybe you've got something here, at that."

The Lieutenant took down Martin's name and address. "You'll hear from somebody," he said, "if this is what I think it is."

Early that evening, as Mrs. Polk and her sons were tuning in on one of their favorite radio programs, the door bell rang. Two courteous gentlemen displayed the credentials of the United States Secret Service. Mrs.

Polk became alarmed. Martin, not wishing to disturb his mother unless it was absolutely necessary, had said nothing to her about the bill or his visit to the police; now, when he explained, Mrs. Polk's alarm passed—to an extent. Who, the mother wondered, had young Bill been associating with to come into possession of fake money that was of official concern to the United States Secret Service?

That was precisely what the Special Agents wanted to know. After talking to Martin, and to Mrs. Polk, and observing Bill, they stated that they were satisfied in their minds that not the slightest suspicion attached itself to the Polk household. Nonetheless, the clue that could lead to a dangerous counterfeiter might reside right in that household—through young Bill. For there was no doubt that this funny-looking money had been printed from the same plate that had been used to print the face of the counterfeits. Examination of the crudely printed paper in the offices of the Secret Service had established that fact beyond question.

"Bill," asked one of the Special Agents, "who is this lad Red that you say you got this bill from?"

"I play ball with him once in a while. I don't know his name."

Bill said that he had known Red for a year or so, through having seen him after school and Saturdays in a playground about five blocks from home. Red, he said, had been selling the funny-looking money the previous morning, Saturday—five bills for a cent. Bill had bought five and given four of them away to friends he played ball with, and had retained just one—the one that Martin had become excited about that morning.

"When do you think you might see Red again?" asked one of the Special Agents.

"Maybe tomorrow afternoon," said Bill. "I see him almost every day at the playground when the weather is good."

There was nothing that the Special Agents could do until school let out the following afternoon. Then they picked up Bill after classes and accompanied him to the playground. Martin had to work in the department store; he wouldn't know what happened until he got home for dinner.

What did happen was that Bill spotted Red almost immediately after entering the playground with the two Special Agents. "Introduce us to Red," one of the Special Agents instructed Bill. "Say we're friends of yours who would like to buy some funny-looking money from him."

Red, a nice lad about Bill's age, with hair so red that other fellows said it could practically be seen in the dark, looked at the Special Agents and grinned. "Sure," he said, "I got money to sell." He reached into his pocket and pulled out a roll of bills—the same kind of bills he had sold to Bill two days previously. "Where," one of the Special Agents asked Red, "do you get this stuff?" "Oh," said Red, "I print it myself."

"You what?"

"I print it myself," said Red. "I got the thing that you print it from."

One of the Special Agents described to Red what an engraving plate, such as is used in the manufacture of real money, looks like. Red began to nod. Yes, he said, that's what he had. At that point, the Special Agents told Bill Polk that they wouldn't need him any more, at least that afternoon. They would accompany Red, whose correct name was Willard Nichols, to his home to get a look at the plate.

Thanks to the alertness of Martin Polk, and to the long arm of coincidence—a double coincidence that not only had acquainted Martin with the details of the counterfeit in the first place, but had turned up a product from one of the counterfeit plates right in his own home—the United States Secret Service was on the trail of a dangerous criminal who had for months baffled the Service.

The moment the Special Agents laid eyes on the plate from which Red had printed the funny-looking bills they knew they had their case partially solved. For this indeed was the plate—one of two plates, rather—that they desperately wanted. Red had no idea where the other plate was—the plate that had printed the back of the bill. A friend of his, a lad of eleven named Harry Parker, had swapped him the plate for a catcher's mitt two weeks previously. Red, who had gotten a printing set for Christmas the previous year, had applied green ink to the plate, cut white paper the size of bills, and printed the play money that he sold to his friends.

Red's friend, Harry Parker, lived two blocks away. Harry was not at home when Red and the Special Agents went over to his apartment house to talk to him. When he did come home, late for dinner, he didn't get a chance to eat. The Special Agents had too many questions to ask him—and so did his father and mother who, alarmed by the presence of the Secret Service representatives, wanted to know what their son had done.

Harry Parker hadn't done anything that the average lad his age wouldn't have done. There had been a fire in an apartment building near the one where he lived, two weeks previously, and the firemen, in going into the apartment where the blaze originated, had heaved a lot of miscellaneous junk out of the burning apartment into a vacant lot alongside the building. Harry Parker had poked around in the junk the following day and found two copper plates—the one he sold to Red and another one.

Where, the Special Agents wanted to know, was the other plate? Harry still had it; he hadn't done anything with it because it hadn't impressed him as being as interesting as the plate with Lincoln's picture on it. He

produced the plate. Sure enough, it was the plate used in the printing of the back of the baffling counterfeit. A trail that had begun with the alert Martin Polk, and threaded through his brother Bill to Bill's friend Red, and from Red to his friend Harry Parker, had come to an end.

Amateur Sleuth

For more than a year, Jimmy Campbell had done extra chores on his father's farm, and on neighboring farms within fifty miles of Indianapolis, to get the money with which to buy every book he could find on the science of being a good detective. Jimmy wanted to be a detective above all else in the world. In fact, he practically had his career planned at the age of sixteen. He intended to become a member of a big metropolitan police force and he hoped to become a real detective, sooner or later.

109

So Jimmy took advantage of every opportunity he could find to read F.B.I. reports, and otherwise become familiar with the techniques of the detection and apprehension of criminals.

Jimmy had definitely developed an acquaintance with the basic principles of crime detection—where to look for and how to develop fingerprints, the kind of questions to ask people who might know something pertinent to the solution of a crime, how to shadow people, and so on.

Jimmy knew that he would have to wait at least five years, until he was twenty-one, to join a police department—but he had no intention of just keeping his hard-won knowledge stored in his brain until that time, not, that is, if there arose a legitimate opportunity to put it to use. Such an opportunity was to come to young Jimmy Campbell sooner than he had hoped it might.

Jimmy was kidded without mercy by his classmates in high school and by neighboring farmers and friends when they heard about his sleuthing ambition. "Hi'ya, Sherlock Holmes" was a favorite greeting he got at school. One of his teachers, when confronted by a classroom mystery, such as a misplaced book, would say, "We will have to put Detective Campbell on the job." Neighboring farmers, who had known his family for a couple of generations wondered whether Jimmy had been seeing too many movies. But Jimmy never was disturbed by any criticism. He'd grin until his eyes were light-blue slits. He knew what he was doing.

There was one person aside from his father and mother (Jimmy was the only boy in the family, having two younger sisters) who thoroughly appreciated his ambition. That was Don Turner, the hired man. Turner was an open-faced big fellow in his twenties, who had come to work on the Campbell acres a few years before and who had stayed on to be one of the family. "Don't let that kiddin' get under your skin, Jimmy," he would say. "Let 'em call you Sherlock Holmes or anything else they want to. You stick to bein' a detective if you want to."

It was Don Turner himself who became a principal in Jimmy Campbell's first mystery. One bright morning in July, when farm work was at its heaviest, Don Turner, who had fixed up quarters for himself over the milk shed, didn't show up for breakfast. Don must be sick, thought Jimmy. He told his father and mother he'd go and see. What he saw was an empty room, and a bunk that hadn't been slept in.

Don Turner didn't own much in the way of worldly goods, but what he owned had disappeared. There wasn't a thing belonging to Don in his quarters. "I'm surprised at Don," said Jimmy's father, who, when Jimmy hadn't returned to the house, had joined him above the milk shed. "I'd of thought that if he decided to go and work someplace else at least he'd have had given me notice, especially at this time of year when the work's so heavy and help's so short."

Jimmy just stood there biting his lower lip. "You always do that when somethin's on your mind, son," said Mr. Campbell. What Jimmy was thinking, and didn't hestitate to say so, was that Don Turner had not disappeared voluntarily. His father grew slightly impatient. "Why, his bed ain't been slept in and"—the father waved an arm and emcompassed the quarters—"he's packed up everything he owned and taken it with him."

"I can't explain it in words, Dad," said Jimmy. "It's just that Don wasn't the kind of fellow to do a thing like that. Those books I read—they teach you to size up a man's character. Don had a fine character; he'd never do anything sneaky." Jimmy looked around the quarters. "Please don't touch anything, Dad," he said.

Morgan Campbell stared hard at his son. "You'll have to prove it to me," he said and walked away.

If Jimmy was going to work on the mystery of Don Turner's disappearance he would have to do it at night, when he wasn't needed for chores on the farm—chores that would be doubly hard, now that Don was gone. All that day, while he helped his dad in the fields, Jimmy turned his mind back to conversations he had had with Don. Don had been a taciturn sort of fellow, so the conversations had not been very enlightening. Once, though, only a few weeks before, Don had mentioned something about maybe getting married some day—to a pretty waitress who worked in the village.

Jimmy got an early bus to the village that evening. There were only two restaurants and a diner in the village, so his field of investigation was not great. He went into the larger of the two restaurants first. He spoke to the cashier—a kindly man with eyeglasses. He explained who he was, further explained that Don Turner had disappeared, then asked the cashier if he would be kind enough to question the waitresses and find out if any of them knew Don.

One of the waitresses said she knew Don. "Did you know him very well?" asked Jimmy. "Well enough to maybe marry him someday?"

The waitress laughed. "No, not that well, young man. You should speak to Clara Markel in the diner on the edge of town. She's very sweet on Don and has been going steady with him."

Miss Markel was a charming girl of perhaps twenty-two, with soft brown hair and a candid smile. Yes, she admitted to Jimmy between serving customers, she was engaged to Don. What was the matter with Don, though? Miss Markel was good and angry at him. He had had a date to meet her the night before, when she got through work in the diner at ten, but he had not shown up. And he had not communicated with her to explain his absence.

"I thought maybe I had got the nights mixed and

that he would show up tonight," said Miss Markel to
Jimmy. "But now that you say he's disappeared; why,
young man, that's serious! We've got to do something
about it."

Jimmy had learned that people often possess information of value in an investigation, but don't think to
mention it. Skillful questioning is, therefore, necessary.
"Would you mind telling me, Miss Markel," said Jimmy,
"if you and Don planned to do anything special last
night?"

"Well, something special and important was to
happen, if that's what you mean. We were to become
formally engaged."

"You mean Don was going to give you an engagement
ring?"

The waitress nodded.

"May I ask how you knew he was going to give you
the ring last night, Miss Markel?"

"Yes. Don said he would have the ring with him when
he picked me up at ten."

"Did he say anything about where he was going to
get the ring?"

"Now, that you speak of it, he did say something
about picking the ring up on the way to meet me."

Where would Don have picked up an engagement
ring on his way to see Miss Markel? Jimmy had learned
about deduction too. Don wouldn't have had the
opportunity to do much traveling to get the ring between

the time he had left the farm the evening before and the time he had been due to call for the waitress. Thus, he had probably planned to pick up the ring right in the village—at Arpel's, which was the only jewelry store in the immediate region.

Arpel's was closed for the night when Jimmy arrived at this deduction. But he went into a telephone booth, right at the end of the diner, and phoned Jonathan Arpel, proprietor of the store, at his home.

Jimmy's deduction paid off. Mr. Arpel said yes, Don Turner had been in about nine thirty the night before to pick up a diamond ring that he had had on order for several weeks. Mr. Arpel had kept his store open after the usual closing time to wait for Don, who had come to town on the bus that arrived at nine thirty.

"Could you give more details about what the ring looked like?" asked Jimmy. Mr. Arpel, to whom Jimmy explained why he was asking the questions, was glad to oblige. The ring had contained a blue-white diamond, weighing one and one-eighths carats, and had been set in white gold with a small emerald chip on each side of the diamond. The jewel had cost $385. Don, who had previously paid for it, put the box containing the ring in his pocket, and walked out of the Arpel establishment whistling. That had been about a quarter to ten.

Jimmy told Miss Markel what Mr. Arpel had told him. The information developed from the jeweler indicated that Don Turner had vanished, right on the streets of the village, between a quarter to ten, when he had left the Arpel store, and ten o'clock, when he had been due to pick up his fiancée. The diner was less than a ten-minute brisk walk from the jewelry store.

It seemed obvious to the young, unofficial sleuth that a crime had been committed—the crime of robbery. Somebody had known that Don Turner was carrying that valuable ring and had taken it from him. But where had the crime been committed and where was Don Turner now?

Miss Markel had begun to cry and some of the patrons in the diner were wondering what was up. "Don't worry," Jimmy assured her, "I'll find out what happened last night."

Jimmy had a feeling that he should report the whole thing to the police. In fact he intended to do so. But he wished he had more information to make sure Don hadn't had a last minute change of heart, and run away.

Jimmy consulted his watch. It was only nine o'clock now. The last bus that would take him back to the farm left at eleven. He had two hours to devote to the mystery tonight; he would think a little longer, then call the police.

It seemed likely to Jimmy that Don Turner had gone directly from Arpel's store toward the diner. Jimmy went to Arpel's, which was on the same street as the diner only closer to the center of the village, and began to take the route he figured Don had taken. Halfway between Arpel's and the diner, he found himself passing through a block which would have been pitch-dark at the time Don had passed through the block, and which was desolation itself. There was a stretch of uncleared ground, thick with trees, on one side of the street, and on the other side was an abandoned metal factory. Very few persons had reason to pass through that particular block after dark.

The crime detection books had taught Jimmy to put himself in the shoes of possible suspects, the better to figure out what they had done. So now he put himself in the shoes of the person or persons, who might have committed the crime. He decided first that the criminal or criminals were not strangers in the village. Rather, they (and Jimmy had the hunch that there had been at least two involved in the crime) knew the village and its inhabitants. They had probably seen Don Turner picking up the ring and followed him. Had the criminals been strangers in town, lingering just long enough to commit a crime, they would not have been likely to follow one individual who made a purchase at Arpel's; they would have been more likely to rob the jewelry store itself.

All right, then. If the criminals were local men, the chances were they had slipped up behind Don Turner and knocked him into unconsciousness. In that way, Don would not have been able to see and recognize them. Jimmy's line of reasoning seemed to be corroborated by the fact that Don's quarters at the farm had been stripped of all his belongings. Only local men would have known where their victim lived; the criminals would have gone to Don's quarters and stripped it to make it look as if Don's disappearance had been voluntary. Thus, with no suspicion aroused, they would have more time to cover their tracks and dispose of their loot in a pawnshop somewhere.

Jimmy stood there, in the deepening gloom of the desolate block, looking with mounting suspicion at the abandoned metal factory. He knew he should call the police, but something impelled him to go inside. He had covered the first floor, without results, and had descended to the basement when he heard a faint sound. It was, he knew, the sound of a human being, a man in pain.

That was how Jimmy Campbell found Don Turner. Don, the man who had told him not to waver in his ambition to be a detective, had been slugged about the head to within a whisper of death.

Jimmy raced out into the street and stopped the first man he found. He told the man what he had discovered in the abandoned factory, and the man rushed to the nearest phone and called the county hospital. The doctors who came said that Jimmy had arrived at the factory none too soon. Don Turner had lost much blood; had Jimmy not found him when he did, it was doubtful if Don would have lived through the night.

Don was in no condition to be questioned in detail. He did say enough, however, to Sheriff Harold Cross to verify Jimmy's reconstruction of the crime. He had been hit from behind and knocked unconscious. He had no idea who had hit him.

Now that the case was in the hands of the duly constituted authorities, Jimmy Campbell was out of it—almost. The ring turned up in an Indianapolis pawn shop the following day. It had been pawned by a fellow with red hair. That was all the pawnbroker knew about the criminal: he had red hair. Such a description could have fitted many people.

But Jimmy Campbell knew something the authorities didn't know. The criminals, in going to Don Turner's quarters and taking their victim's belongings to create the impression that Don had left voluntarily, had handled many objects.

Jimmy looked around Don's quarters, trying to figure out just what the criminals had touched and left their prints on. They had, he decided, touched the plastic knobs of a dresser where Don had kept his clothes; the dresser drawers, emptied, had been open when Don's disappearance had been discovered. A good thing, mused Jimmy, that he had asked his folks not to touch anything in the room.

Jimmy had developed fingerprints many a time with a fingerprint kit his dad had given him for a Christmas present. But this was too important a case for him to take a chance on; he would leave the development of these prints to the authorities. He informed his father of the potential value of an examination of the dresser drawer knobs and Mr. Campbell telephoned Sheriff Cross. The Sheriff, who himself had taken a course in crime detection at the F.B.I. in Washington, went out to the Campbell farm and removed the drawers.

The knobs were heavy with prints—the prints of two men. Sheriff Cross sent the impression to the F.B.I. Laboratory in Washington, where the prints of countless thousands of men with criminal records are on the file. Back came the answer: The prints were those of William (Red) Hawkins and Ed (Big Ed) Wilkinson, men with criminal records who lived only two miles from the village where the crime was committed. Both Hawkins and Wilkinson had been released from prison less than a year previously, and had been presumed to have reformed.

On the basis of the prints developed on the knobs, turned over to the Sheriff through the sleuthing of Jimmy Campbell, Hawkins and Wilkinson were picked up at their homes. They denied their guilt. The pawnshop proprietor in Indianapolis, however, made a positive identification of William (Red) Hawkins as the man with red hair who had, the day after the crime, pawned the ring taken from Don Turner. In the face of the identification, Hawkins confessed, implicating his partner, Wilkinson. Wilkinson had been in the post office the morning of the crime when Arpel the jeweler had received the ring through the registered mails, opened it and remarked to the postmaster that Don Turner was calling at his shop for it that night. Both men were sent to prison.

Don Turner recovered and returned to his work on the Campbell farm. Jimmy Campbell is twenty now. He has a year to go to fulfil the first official step of his life's ambition—to take his examinations for patrolman. On the basis of his perfomance in the mystery of the disappearance of Don Turner, there is little doubt that he will make a fine patrolman—and an even better detective.

Voices from the Grave

Sergeant Harry Storey of the Ontario Provincial police was a tall, lean fellow of reflective bent. Patrolling the Ottawa-Montreal Highway, he compiled a wide assortment of information about people and places and stored it away in his mind. When Storey returned to his patrol job on March 28, 1932, after a month's absence due to illness, and heard that a young farm worker named Leon Bergeron had been trampled to death by two horses ten days previously, he reached into his mental file.

Storey didn't like what he pulled out of that file. Leon Bergeron's death didn't make sense. Bergeron had had a way with horses. He had groomed them, tended them when they were sick and talked to them in a language they seemed to understand.

The scene of Leon Bergeron's death was the farm of a man named François Larocque in the bleak French-Canadian agricultural country near the hamlet of L'Orignal in the northeastern part of Ontario Province. The tillers of the region were hard-bitten men who labored seven days a week, with time out only for church on Sundays, wresting a living from the reluctant soil. They were a highly superstitious lot, too, these farmers, firm believers in ghosts and voices from the dead.

François Laroque, a good-natured, roly-poly man with a shape like a top, was plunged into deep gloom, distraught over the fatal accident on his farm, when Sergeant Storey stopped by to get a first-hand account of the tragedy. "Come to the barn," Larocque said to Storey, "and I'll show you where it happened."

There were two horses in a single stall in the barn. The stall was boarded up on three sides, so that the only entrance to or exit from it was through a door that opened outward into the barnyard. There was a window in this door—a window that also opened outward. The door itself was opened and closed by a latch that could be operated from the inside or the outside.

"Leon must have done something to make the horses wild," Larocque said to Storey, "and they trampled him."

"But he was a pretty quick fellow," said Storey. "Odd that he didn't bolt from the stall when the beasts went mad the way they did."

Larocque figured that the wind had blown the door of the stall closed and that the horses had knocked Bergeron down and begun trampling him before he could reach the latch.

Storey peered into the stall. He noticed that each horse bore a dozen or more tiny scabs on its sides. The scabs were comparatively small, as if the result of flesh punctures of some kind.

Leon Bergeron had not been a regular hand on François Larocque's farm. He had been regularly employed on the farm of a man named Pierre Morin, about a mile down the road. Morin had occasionally hired the boy out to other farmers who were pressed for help. So Sergeant Storey decided to have a talk with Morin.

Morin was a tough customer—a stunted, wiry character who cocked his head and squinted at people when he talked. He had, Storey knew, long been fighting a delaying action with the wolf at the door. Storey wanted to know from Morin the circumstances under which Bergeron had been loaned to Larocque before the fatal accident.

"He wanted the boy to help with his threshing," Morin said to Storey.

"His threshing? You sure of that?"

"What do you mean, am I sure?"

"Are you sure it was threshing that Larocque wanted Bergeron to help out with?"

"Sure I'm sure. I needed the boy myself, but when Larocque come to me and said he was in need of help bad, I let the boy go for a couple of days. And he never come back."

Sergeant Storey pulled his pipe from his pocket, filled it and lit up. He had noticed, while at Larocque's farm, that there was quite an accumulation of threshing work to be done. Thus it seemed unlikely that young Bergeron had done much threshing.

That night, Storey waited until the lights in Larocque's farmhouse were out. Then he stole into the barn where the two horses were stabled. Now, with a flashlight, Storey took a better look at the scabs on the animals. He observed that these marks were in a row and an equal distance apart.

Storey poked around the barn until he found a pitchfork. Now he went to the stall with the implement. The scabs were exactly the same distance apart as the tines of a pitchfork!

The pitchfork was old. Storey closely examined the tines for possible signs of blood. He found none.

There were several splotches that looked like dried blood on the lower part of one of the stall walls. Storey took a penknife, cut away the splotched wood, and put it in his pocket for future examination.

Next night, Storey decided to look around Morin's barn. The first thing that arrested his attention was a pitchfork. It was brand-new, its metal gleaming and its wooden handle hardly soiled.

So Morin had bought a new pitchfork. What, then, had become of his old one? Instinct impelled Storey to climb to the loft of the barn. There, under a small pile of hay, he found a pitchfork handle. Just the handle. The metal end had been removed.

Sergeant Harry Storey now saw, in his mind's eye, the commission of a heinous crime. He could see a man standing outside that door leading into the horse stall on the Larocque farm. He could see the man poke a pitchfork through the window in the stall door, jabbing the screaming horses. And he could see Leon Bergeron, in there with the horses, being trampled to death.

There was one thing Storey could not see—the face of the man with the pitchfork.

Storey drove to Toronto and there walked into the office of Inspector William H. Stringer of the Criminal Investigation Department of the Provincial Police. Inspector Stringer, a tall, austere man with graying hair and a big black moustache, listened in silence as Storey unfolded the facts that led him to suspect Leon Bergeron had been murdered. "It is that man—Morin," Stringer said easily.

Storey had his doubts that Morin was the murderer. "Seems to me," he said to Stringer, "that it would be un-

127

natural for a man to use a pitchfork in a crime a mile from his house and then, with the pitchfork stained with blood, carry the tool all the way home, detach the handle and dispose of the other end."

Inspector Stringer didn't agree. Murderers, he pointed out, were often so emotionally unbalanced after the commission of a crime that they did stupid, unnatural things. Morin, the inspector thought, could very well have gone to Larocque's barn and there killed Bergeron, the plot being that if the murder were discovered Morin would not be suspected.

Bergeron's body was secretly disinterred. Death had been caused when the horses had crushed the youth's head. The body bore other marks—small, round marks the same distance apart as the tines of a pitchfork. The splotches of blood that Storey had retrieved from the murder stall turned out to be type AB.

"Storey," said Inspector Stringer, "you've uncovered a murder. Now you'll have to solve it. You know the people and the background as nobody else on the force does."

What, Storey wondered, could the motive have been for murdering an obscure, impoverished farm hand? Vengeance? No. Removal of an obstacle? Hardly.

Hard cash? How could anybody have gained in a material way from the murder of a youth who had owned nothing but the shirt on his back? How? Why, through insurance! That was how!

Within a week Storey had replies to his queries of Canadian insurance companies, and from American companies with branches in the Dominion. Nobody had taken out insurance on the life of Leon Bergeron.

Really behind the eight-ball now, Storey began to backtrack into the life of the victim, there hoping to find a telltale pointer.

Before going to work for Morin, Leon Bergeron, an orphan, had lived in the boardinghouse of a woman named Louvina Desjardens, in a place called L'Orignal. Madame Desjardens, a woman with a dragon-like face, remembered Bergeron well. While boarding with her, the youth had worked as a handyman in L'Orignal. Then one day a man had called at her establishment looking for somebody to do farm work, so Bergeron had gone away with the man.

Who had that visitor been? His name had been Morin—Pierre Morin. Morin, the man on whose farm Bergeron had been working when Larocque had borrowed the youth, had had a perfect right to meet Bergeron somewhere and offer him a job on his farm. Nothing suspicious in that.

But the ferret in Storey impelled him to keep questioning Madame Desjardens about the departure of Bergeron. "Well," replied Madame Desjardens, "Pierre Morin must have badly needed help on his farm because of his physical condition."

"His physical condition?"

Madame Desjardens looked hard at the officers. "You know Pierre?"

"Slightly."

"Well, you must know he is a hunchback with a short leg."

"I know nothing of the kind. Let us be certain we are talking about the right man." Madame Desjardens described Pierre Morin as middle-aged, small, wiry and, of course, hump-backed and short-legged. Most certainly the woman was not describing Pierre Morin. Or, for that matter, François Larocque, the man on whose farm Bergeron had been murdered. Was the arch-plotter, whoever he was, using Pierre Morin's name?

"You keep calling this Monsieur Morin by his first name," Storey said to the landlady. "Did you know him before that day when he came to take young Bergeron away?"

Indeed, Madame had known the man before that day. She had first met the hunchback when he had called at her boardinghouse one day in the late summer of 1930 —a year and a half before the day he had come for Leon Bergeron.

On the occasion of the hunchback's first call he had also been searching for a youth to do chores on his farm. And so he had made a deal with another young man, who had gone off with him in much the same manner as, later, Leon Bergeron had.

Storey had quite a time poking around Madame Desjardens' memory to come up with the name of the first youth who had gone away with the hunchback. The boy's name had been Anathane Lamarche.

Storey wondered if Anathane Lamarche, too, had met with a fatal accident. The records of the Provincial Police revealed that Lamarche sure as heck had. Lamarche had been drowned in the Ottawa River a year and a half previously.

Lamarche had been drowned while working as an ice cutter. There had been no eyewitnesses to the drowning. But Lamarche's employer, a thoughtful man, remembered young Lamarche well. "He was a nice boy," the employer told Storey, "but he drank heavily. His uncle thought that young Lamarche got drowned because he was drunk."

"His uncle? What was his uncle's name?"

"Morin, as I remember. Pierre Morin."

"Describe him."

The man described a hunchback with a short leg.

"How did you come to know his uncle?"

"The man brought the boy to me and asked me to give him work."

"Did you ever see the boy drunk?"

"No."

"In other words, you had only the uncle's word for it?"

"Yes."

"Where did the uncle live?"

VOICES FROM THE GRAVE

"I never found out."

"Then how did you notify him when the boy was drowned?"

"I didn't have to. He was here visiting the boy."

Visiting indeed!

Sergeant Storey, although he had started out to investigate the death of Leon Bergeron, now found himself concentrating on the death of Anathane Lamarche. For he was now convinced that somewhere in the Lamarche riddle he would find the key to the Bergeron mystery.

Storey soon came upon a most interesting chunk of information. Young Lamarche not only had *not* been drunk, but had been a total abstainer.

Lamarche's body was exhumed. Although decomposition had set in, one thing remained obvious: Lamarche's skull had been fractured. He had been dealt a terrific blow on the back of the head, then tossed into the river.

Anathane Lamarche had been insured with the Dominion Indemnity Company for $5,000 six weeks before his death. The policy had carried a clause specifying double indemnity in case of accidental death.

Lamarche's drowning had been recorded as accidental. Thus the sum of ten grand had been paid to his beneficiary.

The beneficiary had been the boy's father, Felix Lamarche, a farmer.

Storey hung around Felix Lamarche's farm, studying

the old man through powerful field glasses. He sized him up as a none-too-bright character. Old Felix's little farmhouse was a ramshackle lean-to, and the bones of his two horses and three cattle were practically sticking through their skins. Either Felix Lamarche had hidden that insurance money after receiving it, or he had turned it over to somebody else. To the hunchback?

When taking out the insurance policy, old Felix Lamarche had, the company records disclosed, paid for it in cash—$62.50 for one year of the premium. From all Storey had been able to deduce from a study of old Lamarche, the farmer would not have had the cash or the inclination to fork out $62.50 for insurance.

Now Storey addressed himself to an examination of Felix's account at the Royal Bank in the near-by village of Navin. For several years prior to his son's death, Felix had never carried more than $25. The old boy had deposited the ten-grand insurance check one day and, a week later, after the check cleared, had withdrawn the entire sum in cash. Interesting.

Where, Storey wondered, had Felix Lamarche obtained the $62.50 in cash with which to pay the first premium on his son's life? Since there was an obvious tie-up between the deaths of Anathane Lamarche and Leon Bergeron, Storey decided to examine the bank accounts of the two men who had been associated with Bergeron's employer, and François Larocque, on whose farm Bergeron had been murdered.

134

Both Morin and Larocque had accounts in the same bank where old Felix banked. Storey saw, when he examined Morin's small account, that the man had not deposited or withdrawn any money for more than two years. That seemed to deal him out of the picture right then and there.

Larocque, however, had made a withdrawal the day before the first premium had been paid on Lamarche's life a year and a half previously. The withdrawal had been $39—$23.50 short of the sum of $62.50 which had been paid for the first premium. That $39 withdrawal, Storey noticed, had left Larocque a balance of only $1 in his account.

As he sat behind the tellers' cages in that little bank in Navin, there appeared in Storey's mind the figure of Larocque's closest friend—a farmer by the name of François Lavictoire, who lived about halfway between Larocque's farm and that of Pierre Morin. Lavictoire was middle-aged, small and wiry—a description which partially tallied with that of the man who had called at the L'Orignal roominghouse, either hunchbacked or short-legged.

However, Lavictoire's bank account would also bear looking into. And when Storey looked into that bank account, guess what he found? He found that Lavictoire had withdrawn $23.50 the very same day that Larocque had withdrawn $39. And so when he left the bank Sergeant Storey knew that he had brought not one but two killers into the sights, for not one but two murders.

Lavictoire, Storey felt, had been the hunchback using the name of Pierre Morin, and had twice appeared in the roominghouse in L'Orignal. Drawing on his knowledge of the region, Storey now recalled that Lavictoire was something of an amateur actor. The man had, Storey had heard, appeared in church plays in L'Orignal.

One night, when everybody in Lavictoire's house was asleep, Storey took a long chance. He let himself into the house and, flashlight in hand, began to rummage around the first floor. Eventually he came to a desk. In one of the desk drawers was a pile of miscellany.

It was while sifting through the miscellany that Storey found what he had come for. It was the program of a church play that had been performed some three years previously. There was Lavictoire down on the program, playing the part of a hunchback! That explained practically everything.

Now Storey had another inspiration. Perhaps, when the police had first inquired if Leon Bergeron had been insured, and the insurance companies had answered in the negative, there had been a clerical slipup in one of the insurance offices. And now, when the Provincial Police sent follow-up inquiries to the insurance companies about Leon Bergeron, it developed that there surely had been a clerical slipup.

Leon Bergeron had been insured by François Larocque six weeks before his death. Larocque was down on the insurance books as the youth's uncle. The policy had been for $5,000, with double indemnity in case of accidental death. Then, when the horses had trampled Bergeron to death, the insurance company had forked over $10,000 to Larocque.

Storey decided that his next move would be to crack one of the key figures in the case. Since both Larocque and Lavictoire appeared to be hard-shell characters, Storey decided against moving in on them just yet. Old Felix Lamarche, the father of the first insurance victim, looked like a better bet.

Story called on Felix. "I've come to see you about the death of your son," Storey said to the old boy.

"Yes, what about my son's death?"

"Your son wasn't killed in an accident. He was murdered."

"What is that you are saying!"

"I am saying your son was murdered."

Old Felix, who had been standing, sat down. He stared off into space for a while. "I thought something was queer about my boy's death," he said. "I should have known those men weren't giving me that money for nothing."

"Tell me all about it," said Storey.

What had happened was that Larocque and Lavictoire had approached old Felix and told him that they wanted him to insure his son's life; they would pay the premium. If anything should happen to the boy, they told the father, he would be protected because they would let him keep some of the insurance money.

"But why do you wish to insure my son?" old Felix had asked.

"Because," Larocque had answered, "we like the boy like a son and would be at a great loss if anything ever happened to him—such as an accident." Life, Larocque had added, never having spoken truer words, was full of uncertainties. Old Felix, none too quick on the uptake, his mind further dulled by visions of a sum which to him was a fortune, had gone along on the insurance deal.

After his son's death, the two broken-hearted benefactors let old Felix have two thousand of the ten grand. "Don't put it in a bank," they advised. "Banks are not safe." Old Felix, buttoned up to secrecy, had stashed the dough in a fruit jar.

Sergeant Storey made another trip to Toronto to map strategy with Inspector Stringer. The strategy, Storey and Stringer agreed, had better be good, for Larocque and Lavictoire were two genuinely cunning men. They not only had done away with two farm hands and collected insurance, but had also gone to elaborate lengths to point the finger of suspicion away from themselves.

Lavictoire had used the name of Morin, an innocent man, when he had lured the two murder victims from the roominghouse. In the Bergeron murder, either Larocque or Lavictoire had stolen Morin's pitchfork, used it in the crime, then replaced the handle in Morin's barn and buried the fork somewhere.

"I have a plan," Storey said. "Both Larocque and Lavictoire are very superstitious men. They believe in ghosts and voices from the grave—all that sort of thing. I've heard both of them voicing such beliefs in the past. Suppose we get to work on the minds of those two and see if we can't make them lead us to that missing piece of pitchfork."

Day was breaking when Inspector Stringer and Sergeant Storey drove through the Ontario countryside, headed for the murder region. Larocque didn't have a telephone. Lavictoire did. Along toward ten o'clock that night Stringer went into another farmhouse, about midway between Larocque's and Lavictoire's, and asked permission to use the telephone.

Stringer put through a call to Lavictoire's. When Lavictoire answered, Stringer asked him if he would please do him a favor—a matter of life and death. Would he please get into his automobile, drive to Larocque's farm and bring the man back so he could take the

139

call? "I'm calling long distance," said Stringer. "Please hurry."

It was May and the moon was full. Storey, kneeling behind a clump of bushes at the roadside, saw Lavictoire driving toward Larocque's. In a little while, he saw him coming back again.

When Larocque got on the phone, Stringer could tell that he was alarmed. "Hello?" said Stringer, speaking French. "Is that you, François Larocque?"

"Yes! Who is this?"

"This is Leon."

"Leon? Leon who?"

"Don't tell me you have forgotten me so soon, Monsieur Larocque."

"Tell me who this is!"

"It's Leon."

"Leon who!"

"Leon Bergeron."

Stringer could hear Larocque gasping. Then he hung up.

Stringer and Storey started out on foot for a desolate spot that the two plotters would have to pass when Lavictoire took Larocque home. In a little while, as the car containing the murderers approached, Storey and Stringer heaved a log, which they had previously cached, across the roadway. When the car reached the log, the killers got out to remove it.

About a hundred feet back from the roadway, Storey,

in French, cried out: "Help! Help! Let me out of this stall! These horses are killing me!"

Then Stringer let go with a maniacal, blood-curdling laugh.

Both sleuths now stood there listening—listening for some sign of the car starting up again. It didn't. The killers were obviously waiting to hear more.

So the screams started up again. "Help! Let me out of this stall! Stop poking me with that pitchfork! H-e-l-p!" And then the maniacal laugh again.

Silence. In a little while the car started up again.

The following night Stringer telephoned Lavictoire. "Hello," he said. "This is Anathane."

"Who?"

"Anathane."

"Who?"

"Anathane Lamarche." Click.

The following day a letter arrived for Larocque. Printed in block letters, it read:

M. LAROCQUE

MAKE SURE THAT THING IS BURIED MORE THAN TEN FEET. THE POLICE HAVE AN INVENTION THAT WILL DISCOVER IT IF IT IS BURIED LESS THAN—TEN FEET.

A FRIEND

When the letter was delivered, Stringer and Storey, keeping an eye on Larocque's place through field glasses, saw Larocque get into his car. He drove to Lavictoire's. After dark they got into Lavictoire's car and drove to the vicinity of Morin's farm. Getting out of the car, the murderers cut across some fields, one of them carrying a spade. Stringer and Storey tagged along behind. They tailed the pair for about half a mile.

By the light of the moon, one of the killers began to dig. Stringer and Storey were lying in the brush not twenty feet away. Soon they saw the digger reach down into the hole and extract something.

"Now," whispered Inspector Stringer. He and Storey arose and rushed the killers.

There was François Larocque, holding the head of the pitchfork he had stolen from Morin's and used to commit murder.

The insurance money, which the two plotters had cached, was never found, for neither Larocque nor Lavictoire would talk. But Sergeant Harry Storey lost no sleep over that. Storey had started with nothing— absolutely nothing—and here he was, winding up with two fiends on a gallows.

The Other Plot to Kill Lincoln

"Mark my words! Abe Lincoln will never live to reach Washington." The tall man in the back seat of the horse-drawn carriage gave no hint that he had heard the driver's chilling prophecy. As they clip-clopped through the near-silent streets of Philadelphia that night of February 22, 1861, even his craggy face, half hidden under a soft hat, seemed not to change expression. In fact, no one spoke. But the man on his right, Allan Pinkerton, founder of the detective agency that now bears his name, looked grim. On the tall man's left Ward Lamon, a young Illinois attorney, moved protectively closer.

The riders in that carriage knew well what perils lay ahead for the President-elect of the United States during those emotion-torn days before the first guns of the Civil War sounded at Fort Sumter. Pinkerton had learned that in Baltimore, that Maryland hotbed of secessionists, eight men had drawn lots to see which of them would assassinate Abraham Lincoln on his way to his first inauguration in Washington.

A few weeks earlier Pinkerton had arrived in Baltimore on what he thought would be a routine investigation. Officials of the Philadelphia, Wilmington & Baltimore Railroad, the strategic rail link between the North and the South, had asked him to track down rumors secessionists were planning to blow up the steamers that ferried the trains across the Susquehanna River. But within a few days Pinkerton had uncovered a plot of far greater magnitude, one that could change the course of American history.

Pinkerton had immediately set out to gain the confidence of the secessionists who had flocked to Baltimore in an attempt to swing strategically important Maryland to the side of the seven southern states that already had seceded from the Union. Adopting a southern accent and assuming the name "John H. Hutchinson," Pinkerton opened a brokerage office as a cover and established himself as a regular at the bar of Barnum's Hotel, a favorite haunt of the secessionists.

He soon learned that far more was at stake than a few railroad cars. The patrons of Barnum's, their tongues loosened by drink, stated unequivocally that Abraham Lincoln, the newly elected, anti-slavery President, would never reach Washington alive, that he would be assassinated as he passed through Baltimore on Saturday, February 23. One man boasted that he belonged to a group devoted to making certain that Lincoln left Baltimore in a coffin.

Of all the Lincoln-haters, Pinkerton discovered, the most fanatical was Cypriano Fernandina, the hotel's head barber, an Italian immigrant with anarchistic sentiments. Fernandina was busily soliciting funds to charter a steamer on which an escape could be made to the deep South after Lincoln was murdered. When Pinkerton made a handsome contribution, Fernandina invited him to a private discussion in the back room of a saloon near Barnum's. But Pinkerton waited in vain for the barber to divulge the specifics of the plot—exactly how, where, and when Lincoln would be killed—and he didn't dare press the little man for fear of arousing his suspicion.

Leaving Fernandina, Pinkerton went directly to his darkened office, where he met Harry Davies, an operative who had accompanied him from Chicago. Davies, also posing as a wealthy southerner, had just struck up a friendship with an alcoholic Baltimore aristocrat named O. K. Hillard, who claimed that he was receiving telegraphic information on Lincoln's exact movements; these he relayed to an assassination group to which he belonged. When he heard this, Pinkerton immediately concluded that the Hillard group must be tailing the President-elect. The Lincoln party had left Springfield, Illinois, on February 11 and planned to make fifteen goodwill stops before reaching Washington. Presumably the conspirators would flash word of any changes in itinerary to Baltimore.

"Try to join Hillard's conspiracy as quickly as possible," Pinkerton instructed Davies. "I suspect that he and the barber belong to the same group."

The next day Davies confided that he shared Hillard's anti-Lincoln sentiments and wished to become a member of the conspiracy. Hillard said he would see what could be done. A day passed. Two days. Then, only a few short days before Lincoln was due to pass through Baltimore, Hillard told Davies that he was to be sworn into the group.

At eight o'clock that night, Davies met the conspirators, about twenty men from all walks of life, including as Pinkerton had suspected, the barber Fernandina, whom Hillard introduced as "our leader." After swearing Davies into the "cause," Fernandina called the gathering to order. Now, as the head plotter talked and Davies listened, the details of the design for death fell for the first time on unsympathetic ears.

On the following Saturday, Fernandina explained, Lincoln would arrive in Baltimore on the 12:30 P.M. train from Harrisburg, Pennsylvania, and change trains for Washington. Crowds were certain to gather in the narrow station vestibule he would have to walk through, and the conspirators—the men now in the room—would mingle with the crowd. Just before Lincoln entered the vestibule, other secessionists would create a disturbance on the street outside the passageway, thus drawing away the station police. At that moment, the predesignated assassin would step up to the President-elect and either stab or shoot him to death. The chartered steamer would be waiting to take the murderer to the safety of Virginia.

Now, Fernandina said, the time had come to draw lots to determine the identity of the assassin. Holding up a hat, he informed the conspirators that all the ballots in it were white except one. Whoever drew the single red ballot would murder Lincoln. As a precaution against leaks, every man was to keep secret the color of his ballot. No one would know the identity of the assassin until the moment he struck. The lights were then turned off and each man, in turn, reached into the hat.

When the drawing was over (Davies' ballot was white), the tense gathering quickly broke up. Davies, the last of the visitors to leave, was saying good night to his host when something impelled Hillard to take the detective into his confidence. It wasn't true, he said, that the hat contained only one red ballot: it contained eight. The top plotters were taking no chances that their plans might go wrong because one man lost his nerve.

Davies recounted the plot to Pinkerton in the small hours of Tuesday morning, February 19. Trying to arrest the plotters would be useless, Pinkerton knew, because the Baltimore police were largely prosecessionist. Moreover, if action were openly taken against one group of plotters, another could spring up to take its place. The proper strategy, he decided, called for silence, and a counterplot to circumvent the planned crime.

But there was no time to waste. Lincoln's itinerary was tight. He would be in New York City until Thursday, the 21st, when he was to leave for Philadelphia, arriving at 4 P.M. The next day he was scheduled to reach Harrisburg at 2 P.M., and on Saturday morning, February 23, he would head for Washington via Baltimore.

When the Lincoln party reached Philadelphia on Thursday, Pinkerton was waiting, though some hours passed before he could reach attorney Norman Buel Judd, one of Lincoln's closest friends and the troubleshooter for the President-elect's party. When they finally met at the St. Louis Hotel, Pinkerton quickly outlined the Baltimore plot. Judd, alarmed, asked Pinkerton what he thought should be done. Pinkerton glanced at his watch; it was a few minutes after 9 P.M. "There is a Washington car on the last train out of here for Balti-

more at 10:50 tonight," Pinkerton said. "I think Mr. Lincoln should be on it."

In 1861 there were no through trains from Philadelphia to Washington. Washington-bound sleepers were uncoupled at Baltimore and drawn by horses through almost two city streets to the Baltimore & Ohio terminal, where they were coupled to trains heading for the capital. The 10:50 P.M. train out of Philadelphia would reach Baltimore at 3:30 A.M., and the Washington train would depart an hour later.

It was nearly ten o'clock when Pinkerton and Judd reached the hotel where Lincoln and his party were staying, only to find him still receiving the ladies and gentlemen of Philadelphia. Crucial minutes ticked away as the two men waited in an anteroom. Finally the President-elect was able to see them, and the detective quickly described the details of the murder plot to its intended victim.

Lincoln listened impassively, his face devoid of expression, as he interrupted now and then to ask for more details. Then he asked Judd how he thought the situation should be handled. Judd replied that he thought Lincoln, Pinkerton, and he should slip out of the hotel immediately and catch the 10:50 night train to Baltimore.

Lincoln studied the carpet for several minutes. "No," he said at last, "I cannot consent. Tomorrow, Washington's Birthday, I have promised to be at a flag-raising ceremony at Independence Hall and then go on to Harrisburg." He turned to Judd. "If you both think there is real danger in my going through Baltimore openly, I shall try to get away quietly from the people at Harrisburg tomorrow evening. Then I'll place myself in your hands."

Pinkerton worked through the night and well into the next day, perfecting his counterplot. Lincoln was to elude the conspirators by arriving in Baltimore almost half a day ahead of his announced schedule, and leaving for Washington some six hours before the time set for his assassination.

On Friday evening Lincoln was scheduled to have dinner with a few political friends in Harrisburg's Jones House, where he would spend the night. Just as he was sitting down to dinner, a carriage quietly drew up to the side of the inn. Ward Lamon, who had been Lincoln's law partner before the Presidential election, was waiting anxiously at the curbstone. Lincoln, called from the room on the pretext of official business, was able to slip outside unobserved.

Lincoln and Lamon drove off into the darkness, to where a special two-car train was waiting on a siding about two miles outside Harrisburg. They entered the car where four railroad officials, who had been brought into the counterplot, awaited them; the engineer and fireman had no idea that the future President of the United States was aboard. The little special pulled away for its four-hour, hundred-mile trip to get the President-elect back to Philadelphia in time to catch the 10:50 P.M. train for Baltimore. To insure that no spy could pass on information to the plotters, the telegraph lines between Harrisburg and Baltimore had been cut. The run of the special back to Philadelphia was made in total darkness, with oil lamps unlit.

Meanwhile, in Philadelphia Pinkerton was assured by coded telegram that Lincoln was on his way. In a hired carriage, Pinkerton drew up at Pennsylvania Station shortly before Lincoln's special arrived. He instructed the driver to wait nearby while he held a whispered conference with Henry F. Kenney, an official of the line on which Lincoln was to travel to Baltimore.

After the special pulled in, the four men climbed into the waiting carriage, Kenney sitting beside the driver, Lincoln between Pinkerton, and Lamon in the back seat. Normally, the trip across Philadelphia from one station to the other consumed about twenty minutes, and would have brought Lincoln to the other station almost half an hour before departure time. There, he would surely have been spotted by other travelers and possibly by plotters. To kill time, Kenney directed the cab driver up one street and down another, pretending to be searching for someone. It was on this ride that the talkative driver predicted Lincoln's demise, little knowing that Old Abe was at that very moment a passenger in his carriage.

At the almost deserted Philadelphia depot Lincoln assumed a measure of disguise, walking with a stoop and wearing a soft hat instead of his familiar stovepipe. No one even noticed as he entered the rear door of the sleeper, the last car on the train. There was little conversation during the journey. The train pulled into its terminal in Baltimore at 3:30 that Saturday morning, and the Lincoln car was detached and pulled through the streets to be attached to the 4:30 train for Washington.

"The city was in profound repose as we passed through," Pinkerton recorded later. "Darkness and silence reigned." Perhaps even now the holders of the red ballots were nerving themselves for their part in the dreadful work, or tossing upon sleepless couches.

Lincoln reached Washington at 6 A.M. on February 23, but word of his arrival was kept secret until after the train from Harrisburg had reached Baltimore, where the crowd surging in and around the terminal was the largest in the city's history.

Less than two weeks later, on March 4, 1861, Lincoln stood before the unfinished dome of the Capitol. From the notes that he had carried safely through Baltimore, he began his First Inaugural Address: "In your hands, my dissatisfied fellow country-men, and not in mine is the momentous issue of civil war . . ."

On April 12, 1861, the Confederacy answered him at Fort Sumter. And four years later, the man who had steered his country through civil war lay dead at the hand of another dissatisfied fellow countryman, John Wilkes Booth.

Index

155

INDEX

Tobacco tax stamps, 45
Topeka, 69, 73, 77, 78, 80, 81
Toronto, 127, 138
Treasury Building, 35
Turnbull, John, 75, 79, 80
Turner, Don, 111–118, 120–122

United States, 29, 45, 59, 67, 144, 152
United States Forest Products Laboratory, 33, 34
United States mailbox, 26
United States Postal Inspection Service, 21
United States Secret Service, 35–40, 42, 44, 45, 51, 99–102, 104, 105

Valentine, Jimmy, 45
Virginia, 147

Wabaunsee County, Kansas, 72, 73, 75, 78
Walker, Jesse (Jesse Reklaw), 16–19
Walters, Samuel, 10, 14, 17, 18, 20
Washington, D. C., 35, 121, 143, 145–148, 150, 151, 153
Washington Square North, 55, 61, 62
Welch, John, 69–72, 76, 77, 79, 81
Wilkes-Barre, Pennsylvania, 21, 22, 26, 30, 34
Wilkinson, Ed (Big Ed), 121
Willard, Mr. and Mrs. John, 73–77, 80, 81
World War II, 97

Yankee Stadium, 9
Yokohama, 65

The Author

ALAN HYND was born in Trenton, New Jersey. A graduate of Columbia University, he has been an editor and a writer. The author of more than twenty books about crime and criminals, Mr. Hynd has also written many articles for magazines such as *The Saturday Evening Post* and *Reader's Digest*. His books, *Passport to Treason* and *Betrayal from the East,* were nation-wide best sellers in the adult field. GREAT CRIME BUSTERS is his first juvenile.

Mr. Hynd and his wife live in New York City and Westport, Connecticut. They have a daughter, Diane, and a son, Noel.